TEACHER HACKS
LANGUAGES

BY
SILVIA BASTOW & SINÉAD MOXHAM
SERIES EDITOR: MICHAEL CHILES

Together we unlock every learner's unique potential

At Hachette Learning (formerly Hodder Education), there's one thing we're certain about. No two students learn the same way. That's why our approach to teaching begins by recognising the needs of individuals first.

Our mission is to allow every learner to fulfil their unique potential by empowering those who teach them. From our expert teaching and learning resources to our digital educational tools that make learning easier and more accessible for all, we provide solutions designed to maximise the impact of learning for every teacher, parent and student.

Aligned to our parent company, Hachette Livre, founded in 1826, we pride ourselves on being a learning solutions provider with a global footprint.

www.hachettelearning.com

Although every effort has been made to ensure that website addresses are correct at time of going to press, Hachette Learning cannot be held responsible for the content of any website mentioned in this book. It is sometimes possible to find a relocated web page by typing in the address of the home page for a website in the URL window of your browser.

Hachette UK's policy is to use papers that are natural, renewable and recyclable products and made from wood grown in well-managed forests and other controlled sources. The logging and manufacturing processes are expected to conform to the environmental regulations of the country of origin.

To order, please visit www.hachettelearning.com or contact Customer Service at education@hachette.co.uk / +44 (0)1235 827827.

ISBN: 978 1 0360 1065 2

© Silvia Bastow & Sinéad Moxham 2025

First published in 2025 by
Hachette Learning (a trading division of Hodder & Stoughton Limited),
An Hachette UK Company
Carmelite House
50 Victoria Embankment
London EC4Y 0DZ
www.hachettelearning.com

The authorised representative in the EEA is Hachette Ireland, 8 Castlecourt Centre, Dublin 15, D15 XTP3, Ireland (email: info@hbgi.ie)

Impression number   10 9 8 7 6 5 4 3 2 1
Year   2029 2028 2027 2026 2025

All rights reserved. Apart from any use permitted under UK copyright law, no part of this publication may be reproduced or transmitted in any form or by any means, electronic or mechanical, including photocopying and recording, or held within any information storage and retrieval system, without permission in writing from the publisher or under licence from the Copyright Licensing Agency Limited. Further details of such licences (for reprographic reproduction) may be obtained from the Copyright Licensing Agency Limited, www.cla.co.uk

Typeset in the UK.

Printed and bound by CPI Group (UK) Ltd, Croydon, CR0 4YY

A catalogue record for this title is available from the British Library.

TABLE OF CONTENTS

About the authors iv
Foreword v
Acknowledgements vi
Introduction vii

Section 1: The pillars of progression 1
Chapter 1: Phonics and pronunciation 3
Chapter 2: Vocabulary instruction 10
Chapter 3: Teaching grammar 20
Chapter 4: Incorporating culture 27

Section 2: The four language skills 31

Listening
Chapter 5: Decoding and parsing skills 33
Chapter 6: Prediction skills and inferences 38

Speaking
Chapter 7: Role play 43
Chapter 8: Photo card 46
Chapter 9: Conversation 50

Reading
Chapter 10: Reading aloud 53
Chapter 11: Reading comprehension tasks 59
Chapter 12: Translation to English 62

Writing
Chapter 13: Dictation 65
Chapter 14: Photo task 71
Chapter 15: Extended writing task 75
Chapter 16: Translation to target language 81

Section 3: Feedback, assessment and revision 86
Chapter 17: Effective feedback in MFL 88
Chapter 18: Metacognition: preparing for assessments 90
Chapter 19: Revision strategies 98

Section 4: Technology integration 104
Chapter 20: Effective use of technology to enhance learning 105

Conclusion 110
Key terms 111
Bibliography 112

ABOUT THE AUTHORS

Silvia Bastow is the Head of Languages at Ercall Wood Academy in Shropshire, with a specialism in German and over 20 years of experience in secondary education. She is a Specialist Leader in Education (SLE) for MFL, a GCSE examiner, and a Fellow of the Chartered College of Teaching (FCCT). In addition, Silvia regularly mentors both Initial Teacher Education (ITE) trainees and Early Career Teachers (ECTs) and serves as the Honorary Membership Officer (HMO) for the Association for Language Learning (ALL).

She holds a Master's degree in German Linguistics from the University of Prešov (2001) and the National Professional Qualification for Leading Teacher Development (NPQLTD). A passionate advocate for Second Language Acquisition and evidence-informed practice, Silvia frequently presents at educational conferences at local, national, and international levels.

As a German Expert Mentor (GEM) for the Goethe-Institut's GIMAGINE project, she supports departments and teachers across the country in strengthening the provision of German in state secondary schools. She blogs at: www.fraubastowmfl.co.uk.

Sinéad Moxham is an experienced senior leader and former head of languages with over 15 years in education. A qualified linguist and expert in language acquisition, she is passionate about language learning and has a keen interest in school leadership. Sinéad supports the professional development of colleagues nationally, as a facilitator and coach of teachers at all levels, ranging from early career teachers to experienced middle and senior leaders. She believes that no one is ever the finished product and is committed to her own professional development. Sinéad holds the National Professional Qualification for Headship (NPQH).

She brings a wealth of international school expertise and serves as both a GCSE examiner and a global learning ambassador. As a dedicated educator, she champions high-quality education through evidence-informed practice, collaborative inquiry and a deep commitment to cultural integration in the MFL classroom and beyond.

FOREWORD

Teaching is complex, and the cognitive demands are substantial. Teachers are seen as masters of their subject from day 1, but teaching requires 'in the moment' decisions to be made when knowledge and understanding of the intricacies of curriculum design may be imperfect. Teachers need to learn on the job to quickly develop an understanding of the most effective approaches to teaching, and skillfully use these approaches to deliver subject matter to their students in a way that they will understand.

In recent years, schools have invested a lot of time and thought into how we can codify teaching pedagogy so that it creates consistency, clarity and a shared understanding among teachers. By establishing clear, research-informed methods for instruction, schools can ensure that teachers know and can apply effective practices that are easily replicable and adaptable, and that can contribute towards maintaining high standards across diverse classrooms and curriculums. However, despite all the research, we still grapple with views on the best pedagogy approaches, and this can make continuing professional development (CPD) somewhat confusing.

One area of professional development that does not seem to get the same limelight is subject pedagogy development. We often assume that once a teacher is qualified, they can automatically teach their subject. However, the role of subject pedagogy professional development in schools is a crucial part to support teaching and learning, as it contributes towards the unique demands of each subject in the curriculum. Effective subject-specific pedagogy enables teachers to break down complex concepts into more-accessible steps, making it easier for students to grasp challenging material.

In this book, Silvia and Sinéad provide a comprehensive guide on how to approach the teaching of languages in schools. From phonics and comprehension to decoding and parsing skills, this book provides detailed guidance on how you might approach teaching these elements in your classroom.

The aim of this book, as with all the books in the *Teacher Hacks* series, is to provide an insight into a teacher's classroom; a look through the keyhole to see how expert practitioners approach some of the most complex and challenging elements of their subject. In this book, this is exactly what Silvia and Sinéad have done. They use their considerable experience to highlight the challenging aspects of language teaching and share some of their teaching hacks to help others in their classrooms.

Michael Chiles

ACKNOWLEDGMENTS

We would like to extend our heartfelt gratitude to Michael Chiles for providing us with the opportunity to write this book.

Our sincere thanks also go to all our colleagues in the MFL community who have generously shared their ideas and professional insights online, via social media and networking events, providing invaluable advice and input on many of the strategies included in this book.

We would like to thank Claire Wilson for sharing her brilliant 'Flash phonics' activity and Barry Smith for sharing his innovative teaching approach using parallel texts in French. This has provided valuable insights and a unique approach to language teaching. Barry, who works as a consultant in MFL and school culture, can be reached on Twitter/X @BarryNSmith79 or via email at BarryNSmith79@gmail.com.

We also appreciate Hannah Pinkham for her generosity in sharing the successful strategy developed by her and her colleague Verity Howarth in which narratives and stories are incorporated into the teaching of French and Spanish. Our thanks go to Dr Liam Printer for sharing his extensive knowledge and research on Teaching Proficiency through Reading and Storytelling (TPRS), and allowing us to include examples of his stories in this book. Additionally, we thank Dannielle Warren for her idea of text analysis, which significantly enhances students' writing skills, and Jérôme Nogues for his expert contribution to Chapter 20.

Our gratitude also goes to John Rolfe, MBE, a true champion of global education and cheerleader of all in the MFL community. Your passion, drive and commitment to internationalism shines through everything you do, and we are truly thankful.

Your contributions have been invaluable, and this book is a testament to the collective wisdom and innovation of the language teaching community. Thank you!

Finally, we are grateful to our families for their invaluable support throughout the writing process.

Silvia Bastow & Sinéad Moxham

INTRODUCTION

Why have we decided to write this book?

In today's diverse and interconnected world, being able to speak a modern foreign language is a big deal. It is not just about communicating with people from different countries; it is also about opening up a whole new world of opportunities. Whether for travel, work or just to make new friends, knowing another language can be a game-changer. It helps us understand different cultures, communicate better and see things from new perspectives. Plus, learning a language is like giving our brain a workout; it boosts our problem-solving skills and keeps our mind sharp.

As modern languages teachers, we have a powerful influence over our young learners. Beyond conjugating verbs and memorising vocabulary, we hold the key to unlocking their potential as global citizens and future professionals who can speak another language.

Through our guidance and expertise, we not only impart linguistic skills but also instil cultural understanding and communication. By sharing our knowledge and experiences, we broaden their horizons, exposing them to diverse perspectives and traditions from around the world. We empower them to navigate an increasingly interconnected society with confidence and empathy. Our classrooms become places for exploration, where curiosity flourishes and stereotypes dissolve.

Yet, a portion of our learners face challenges when it comes to studying another language. They may fail to see its relevance to their lives or struggle to memorise new vocabulary, grasp complex grammar concepts and master unfamiliar sounds, or simply find it tough in the classroom context to achieve the fluency that would fuel their motivation to keep going in their studies.

Learning a language is mostly an unconscious process, akin to absorbing it naturally while engaging with it. We cannot just simply decide to learn a specific aspect like the past perfect tense in one learning episode. Why? Because our brains prioritise what is most crucial for understanding meaning in communication. When we interact, our brains focus on the elements of language that facilitate comprehension and these are more likely to stick in our memory.

Simply explaining language rules and then practising them does not lead to true language acquisition. Input, or exposure to the language via all modalities, builds the foundation of language acquisition, while output, or practising language skills, helps students access that foundation. Without input, there cannot be any meaningful output.

Studying grammar rules does not equate to actually acquiring the language. Instead, language acquisition happens more naturally through exposure and usage. All languages can be learned through exposure to input, and relying solely on memorising grammar rules is not sufficient. Therefore, input, output, interaction and other elements all play equally important roles in the process of language learning.

However, it is important for us to recognise that we cannot always replicate the natural process of acquiring our first language when it comes to second language acquisition, especially considering the limited classroom time available in school settings. In England, students typically have around two MFL lessons of approximately 60 minutes each per week at key stage 3 (KS3) and five lessons a fortnight at KS4. Given these limitations, we need to explore how we can make the most of our curriculum time to address some of the more challenging concepts that, in the conditions given, might need to be taught in a more explicit way, and that is what we are aiming to explore in this book.

Who is this book for?

This book was written for the teachers of MFL, whether they are novice teachers or expert teachers. It is here to help them tackle what we have identified as some of the trickiest concepts of teaching modern languages when applying an explicit instruction. Although the book is aimed at the secondary sector (KS3 and KS4/learners aged 11–16 years old), there are elements in each section that can also be applied in the primary sector (KS2/learners aged 9–11 years old).

We have included a range of practical hacks and examples as well as case studies which, when applied, can support teachers' day-to-day practice in explicitly delivering these challenging concepts.

We also hope that MFL subject leaders and curriculum leaders will consider implementing and embedding strategies suggested in this book in their subject-specific CPD and T&L (teaching and learning) handbooks.

What do we hope teachers of world languages will take away from this book?

The book is organised so that each of its four sections and 20 chapters not only delves into the principles of second language acquisition (SLA), covering the four language skills (listening, speaking, reading and writing) and what the Ofsted MFL research review (Ofsted, 2021) identifies as the three pillars of progression (phonics, vocabulary and grammar), but also touches on effective assessment, revision strategies, cultural engagement and technology integration to support learning.

Rather than advocating for a specific pedagogical approach or methodology, the aim of the book is to highlight a number of what we view as some of the most effective strategies for explicitly addressing these challenging aspects of language teaching. We hope this book will be a go-to resource for colleagues; one they will return to often as they reflect on their teaching practice.

SECTION 1: THE PILLARS OF PROGRESSION

In November 2016, the Teaching Schools Council (TSC) initiated a comprehensive review of the existing evidence regarding current teaching methods and successful pedagogical approaches in MFL education, with a specific focus on KS3 and KS4. Subsequently, the findings of this review along with a series of key recommendations were released in the 'Modern Foreign Languages Pedagogy Review' (Bauckham, 2016). One of the key recommendations put forward was:

> *Pupils need to gain systematic knowledge of the vocabulary, grammar, and sound and spelling systems (phonics) of their new language, and how these are used by speakers of the language. They need to reinforce this knowledge with extensive planned practice and use in order to build the skills needed for communication.*

Following this review, the key recommendations sparked extensive discussions within teacher education, professional networks and at Ofsted events. The latest Ofsted MFL research review (Ofsted, 2021) mentions one of the identified factors that can enhance a high-quality languages curriculum:

> *The curriculum is carefully planned around logical pupil progression in the '3 pillars' of language: phonics, vocabulary, grammar – and the interplay between them.*

In MFL, the three pillars of progression form a foundational framework for language learning and development. These pillars encompass phonics, vocabulary and grammar, serving as essential building blocks for students to achieve proficiency in their target language.

- **Phonics**, the first pillar, lays the groundwork for accurate pronunciation and auditory comprehension, helping students decode unfamiliar words and sounds.
- **Vocabulary**, the second pillar, expands students' lexical repertoire, enabling them to express ideas and communicate effectively.
- **Grammar**, the third pillar, provides the structural framework necessary for constructing meaningful sentences and understanding the rules of syntax – the nuances of language usage.

Together, these three pillars form a solid foundation upon which students can build their language skills and fluency as well as engage confidently with the target language in various contexts. However, we believe that an integral aspect of this framework should also encompass **culture** and **cultural sensitivity**, which is why we opted to incorporate it into this section.

CHAPTER 1
PHONICS AND PRONUNCIATION

On the first day of the new academic year, Madame El-Sayed steps into her classroom, excited to meet her Year 8 French class. Armed with her passion for teaching, she imagines a year filled with engaging activities, lively conversations and rapid progress in her students' language skills.

However, after just a couple of lessons, Madame El-Sayed finds herself facing unexpected challenges. As she introduces new vocabulary and phrases, she notices a common struggle among her students: pronunciation. Many of them stumble over simple words, their attempts at French sounding more like a mishmash of syllables than coherent language. Moreover, she senses a reluctance and even fear among her students to speak out. They seem hesitant to participate in class activities, preferring to stay silent rather than risk mispronouncing words or sounding foolish in front of their peers.

Madame El-Sayed can see the frustration in their eyes as they struggle to grasp the unfamiliar sounds of the French language. As she tries to engage her students in activities, Madame El-Sayed finds them disengaged and unmotivated. Their lack of enthusiasm for learning French is palpable, and she wonders what she can do to ignite their interest in the language and culture she loves so much. Beyond the surface-level challenges of pronunciation and participation, Madame El-Sayed detects a deeper issue: her students' self-efficacy is at an all-time low. They lack confidence in their ability to learn French, convinced that they will never master the language no matter how hard they try. This lack of belief in themselves only serves to further hinder their progress and enthusiasm for the subject.

Unfortunately, this is a situation that is all too familiar in a number of language classrooms, where the explicit teaching of phonics, and consequently pronunciation, has not always been prioritised.

While mastering a new language is a multifaceted and complex process, with its various components intricately intertwined, within the domain of MFL education, the significance of phonics instruction cannot be underestimated. Phonics, the method of teaching the correlation between sound and symbol (spelling) correspondences (SSC), serves as a foundational tool for language acquisition, that enables learners to decode (sound out words/convert graphemes to phonemes) and encode (spell the words/convert phonemes to graphemes) new sounds, fosters improved pronunciation and word recognition, and develops their reading and writing skills effectively, assisting in the development of overall language competence.

Direct and systematic teaching of phonics, while traditionally associated with acquisition of reading and spelling skills in the context of learners' native language, has transcended linguistic boundaries and is now recognised as a crucial component of teaching MFL and is classed as one of the three pillars of progression, providing learners with a structured approach to mastering the intricacies of pronunciation and spelling in a new linguistic context. As the Ofsted MFL research review (Ofsted, 2021) puts it:

> ... teaching needs to explicitly draw attention to phonics (sounds and script) to ensure that language learning is as efficient as possible for as many learners as possible ...

In this chapter, we will explore the rationale and strategies for integrating phonics instruction into MFL curricula. Drawing upon evidence-informed practice, we will navigate the theoretical foundations that support the efficacy of phonics education in MFL, highlighting its capacity to enhance and cultivate learners' linguistic proficiency and fluency. Additionally, we will examine practical considerations for implementing phonics instruction in MFL classrooms. We will present specific examples of strategies – useful hacks – for implementing phonics instruction in classroom practice in an explicit manner.

What are the reasons for teaching phonics?

Systematic and embedded teaching of phonics contributes to the advancement of both oracy and literacy. Nonetheless, using phonics as part of MFL teaching, which encompasses 'phonological awareness' defined by Woore (2022) as 'the ability to recognize, identify, or manipulate any phonological unit within a word', differs from teaching phonics in the learners' first language (L1). In the context of learning a second language (L2), beginners face a substantial cognitive challenge as they need to comprehend the pronunciation, written form and meaning of words simultaneously.

The research shows that many L2 learners attempt to decode unfamiliar words phonetically while reading. This can be beneficial for various aspects of language learning including reading comprehension. Learners' ability to decode accurately in the L2 can also facilitate vocabulary acquisition, promote learner autonomy, aid in grammar learning (such as distinguishing between '*je*' and '*j'ai*' or *'parle'* and *'parlé'*), as well as enhance motivation and improve skills in speaking, listening and writing. A number of studies conducted in UK MFL classrooms, primarily focusing on L2 French – including Erler & Macaro (2011), Woore (2009), Macaro (2007) and Hamada & Koda (2008) – also indicate that in the absence of explicit instruction:

- students demonstrate limited proficiency in phonological decoding
- students may recognise that words should be pronounced differently from English but lack clarity on the correct pronunciation
- their progress in this skill appears to be limited
- English spelling-to-sound associations persist firmly.

So, where do we begin?

When devising our curriculum, it is important to consider the languages being taught and their complexities. Teaching French phonics, for instance, poses greater challenges compared to German or Spanish phonics.

How do we decide which phonemes/graphemes to introduce and when? Should we prioritise silent letters in French to aid in other areas of language acquisition, such as grammar and teaching present tense forms?

Factors such as frequency, difficulty level or the expertise of the teacher may also come into play. It is equally important to ensure that these targeted phonemes are systematically revisited in all speaking, listening and reading activities when teaching a particular topic, rather than solely focusing on individual words. Phonics instruction, decoding skills and practice should be integrated into every lesson, rather than treated as a separate activity. This can be achieved effortlessly in class in every task we present. Using mini whiteboards can be highly effective, allowing teachers to instantly observe students' progress and identify any gaps in their knowledge. Integrating phonics into context might involve beginning with individual sounds, then segmenting and blending them to form complete words, ultimately progressing to reading full sentences.

 ## HACK #1

5 minutes practice: The teacher presents a sound /word in the target language (TL), and students either say it aloud or they can construct and say a full sentence – focus can be on specific phonemes related to the lesson objectives or on incorporating and recycling previously learned SSC. This strategy can be used as a choral response or a teacher might decide to use the 'cold call' technique to target specific learners.

Flash phonics: French			
	Nous avons	qu	J'aime
bleu	ça		college
	trois	quitter	travailler

Activity idea: Claire Wilson

HACK #2

Phonics bingo: The teacher reads either single words or full sentences, providing students with opportunities to practise the decoding of SSC on mini whiteboards or printouts, introducing an element of competition. The use of mini whiteboards is particularly effective because it allows teachers to quickly gauge the proficiency of students' decoding skills.

Phonics bingo: Spanish			
gente	hermano	guitarra	cine
nueva	chica	equipo	voy a
juego	quiero	gato	perro
pero	cumpleaños	hice	belleza

HACK #3

Mind reader: The teacher secretly writes a phrase on a piece of paper and students take turns guessing the phrase aloud. This activity can also be done by students in pairs, while the teacher moves around the class, listening to students' pronunciation.

Mind reader: Spanish
1. Fui a Alemania.
2. Fuimos al cine.
3. ¿Fuiste de vacaciones?
4. Mis padres fueron a España.
5. Hice natación.
6. Hicimos deberes.
7. ¿Hicisteis equitación?
8. Mi hermano hizo vela.
9. Vi una película, fue genial.
10. Vieron una película de terror.

Activity idea: Dr Gianfranco Conti

HACK #4

Minimal pairs: The teacher reads a word aloud, and students use mini whiteboards to write down the corresponding word number, practising decoding skills. This activity could also be modified by presenting minimal pairs in two columns; students must determine which column each word belongs to by writing it down.

Minimal pairs: German			
1.	sehe	11.	weil
2.	sehr	12.	viel
3.	gehe	13.	Weile
4.	gern	14.	viele
5.	Wien	15.	für
6.	Wein	16.	vier
7.	Kiste	17.	Zahl
8.	Küste	18.	Saal
9.	Biene	19.	frisch
10.	Beine	20.	frech

Minimal pairs: French	
moules	mules
déjà	des chats
du vent	du vin
les grands	l'écran
faux	feux
bout	but
russe	rousse
pâte	patte
mes	mais
vie	vue

HACK #5

Link up!: Students listen to the teacher reading sentences out loud and link up words/chunks by identifying the correct SSC.

1. Ich habe einen Bruder.
2. Meine Brüder sind sehr groß.
3. Er geht gern ins Kino.
4. Wie irre!

Link up!

 MORE HACKS

Additional activity ideas might involve a range of reading-aloud exercises, including reading full sentences, omitting letters and presenting only initial letters to heighten challenge levels. Gap-fill exercises, where students fill in individual letters for complex and tricky SSC, completing sentences with full words, providing phonetic spellings of words for students to highlight correct pronunciation, and more, can be effective. Such activities serve to strengthen pronunciation, decoding skills and SSC understanding simultaneously.

Conclusion: Does teaching phonics in a second language yield positive outcomes?

Research on the impact of teaching phonics in MFL is still in its early stages. However, the existing studies, primarily focused on L2 French and English, consistently indicate that phonics instruction can lead to positive outcomes in L2 phonological decoding.

The research evidence on this question remains limited in quantity, and the studies that do exist have various methodological limitations. However, consistently positive effects of phonics instruction on L2 decoding have been found across various phases of formal education (primary school, secondary school and university). It appears that L2 learners who are taught phonics are more likely to develop more accurate SSC knowledge than those who are not. Experimental evidence is also emerging of an impact on L2 vocabulary learning (Woore, 2022).

CHAPTER 2
VOCABULARY INSTRUCTION

> It's May, and Toni's Year 7 Spanish class has been studying the language since September. With every lesson, Toni finds herself more captivated by Spanish. The rhythm of the words, the melody of the phrases – she's hooked. But as the months pass by and the vocabulary starts piling up, she is also hit with a challenge she hadn't quite anticipated: remembering it all. It's not just Toni who's feeling the weight of the expanding lexicon. Many of her classmates are in the same boat. At first, it was manageable. Learning the basics felt like unlocking a new world. But now, as the vocabulary and new sentence structures build upon each other, they are starting to feel the strain.
>
> Their teacher, Señor Morales, assigns vocabulary homework every week. It's supposed to help reinforce what they've learned in class. And it does … to an extent. But lately, Toni's noticing something troubling. Words from previous topics keep cropping up in new lessons, and she is struggling to keep understanding them all. Each week, the list of words to remember grows longer. Some of them are easy to remember – they are the ones they use every day in class. But others slip away, lost in the shuffle of new information. And when those forgotten words come up in later lessons, Toni can feel the frustration building up inside her. Toni loves Spanish; she really does. But as the school year progresses, she can't shake the nagging worry that she is falling behind. She wants to excel in her language studies; to feel confident expressing herself in Spanish.
>
> As she sits at her desk, staring at yet another set of new words, Toni can't help but wonder: Is there a better way to learn? Is there some secret technique she's missing; some magic formula that will make it all click into place?

As we can observe in Toni's case, acquiring vocabulary presents a challenge for our learners. This is partly due to the scale of the task and partly due to the diversity of vocabulary types to be mastered, making knowing a word quite complex. In modern language learning, vocabulary instruction is like the fuel that powers our language engine. However, there is a distinction between learning vocabulary as a native speaker and as a second-language learner. Research suggests that intentional learning is more efficient and leads to better recall, particularly in the earlier stages of language learning, resulting in improved short- and long-term retention.

What does it mean to truly know a word?

Words are primarily learned based on how frequently we encounter them and how thoroughly we process them. While we often acquire new vocabulary implicitly through exposure, explicit vocabulary instruction can enhance learning by supporting internal processing. Vocabulary expert Professor Paul Nation (2013) provides a concise overview of three areas involved in knowing a word: form, meaning and use.

Fundamentally, knowing a word means recognising it in both speech and writing, which involves identifying its **form**. At a receptive level, this includes recognising what the word sounds like and looks like. At a productive level, it involves knowing how to pronounce and spell the word. However, word knowledge extends beyond mere recognition. Students must also understand a word's **meaning**, including both its literal and associative meanings. Additionally, knowing a word involves **using** it appropriately in communication, understanding its grammatical function and knowing the contexts in which it is appropriately used.

When assessing vocabulary proficiency, we should also consider various dimensions beyond the sheer number of vocabulary items. Professor James Milton (2009) divides word knowledge into three components: **breadth**, referring to the number of words students know; **depth**, indicating how well they understand those words and the extent of their knowledge about them; and **fluency** (or automaticity and speed of recall), which denotes how easily they can use these words in both comprehension and production. Recent developments in vocabulary assessment also include the verb lexicon.

Another aspect to consider is the distinction between the vocabulary we want students to actively use in their speaking and writing and the vocabulary they should merely recognise and understand without necessarily using themselves. Students frequently experience frustration when they understand more than they can produce yet; clarifying the concept of **productive** (active) versus **receptive** (passive) vocabulary knowledge as a typical aspect of learning can offer reassurance.

How many words do students need to know?

The number of words students might need to know varies based on the language being studied and the desired level of proficiency. This requirement differs between spoken and written language, where optimal comprehension necessitates a 98% comprehensible input (CI). Milton (2009) writes that:

> Knowing less than 1000 words of a foreign language is probably insufficient for comprehension, even in spoken language, unless

communication is of the most formulaic kind, such as greetings, and lacking in any specific or specialised content.

The *Modern Foreign Languages Pedagogy Review* (Bauckham, 2016) highlights that, 'Vocabulary selection should be informed by frequency of occurrence'. The new GCSE specification similarly underscores the importance of teaching targeted word lists derived from high-frequency lexicons.

Following the review, the National Centre for Excellence in Language Pedagogy (NCELP) – funded by the Department for Education (DfE) – was launched in 2018. This initiative introduced lexical profiling software, the MultilingProfiler (University of York, n.d.), to determine the vocabulary that should be prioritised for teaching and inclusion in examinations. Regardless of becoming entangled in the specifics of the new GCSE specification, it's evident that there exists a substantial correlation between the breadth of vocabulary and the proficiency level of learners. As Milton (2013) put it:

Generally speaking, the more words a learner knows, the more they are likely to know about them, and the better they are likely to perform, whatever the skill.

Research indicates that effective vocabulary acquisition entails a combination of **explicit** (deliberate teaching) and **implicit** (unintentional learning) methods through exposure to CI.

Mastering vocabulary largely revolves around retention, requiring students to encounter, vocalise and write newly acquired words repeatedly before confidently claiming to have learned them: 'Multiple exposure and use are important to consolidate knowledge and develop fluency, anywhere between 5–16 encounters' (Nation, 2001).

Recycling is necessary, and if it is neglected, many partially learned words will be forgotten, wasting all the effort [...] Recycling has to be consciously built into vocabulary learning programs, and teachers must guard against presenting lexical items once and then forgetting about them, or else their students will likely do the same.

(Schmitt, 2008)

Professor Paul Nation's 'The four strands' (Nation, 2007) serve as a valuable framework for integrating vocabulary instruction into the curriculum.

- **Meaning-focused input** – offering abundant spoken and written CI
- **Meaning-focused output** – providing opportunities for speaking and writing practice

Chapter 2 VOCABULARY INSTRUCTION

- **Language-focused learning** – encouraging learners to contemplate the forms of the language, such as relationships between nouns, adjectives and verbs.
- **Fluency development** – allowing learners opportunities to enhance their retrieval speed.

How can we support our students with vocabulary learning?

As Barcroft (2019) argues, one of the most significant disadvantages of learning single words in isolation is that this approach fails to provide learners with the language-specific meanings, uses and collocational properties necessary for truly knowing a word. Teaching and learning vocabulary in context rather than as isolated words can enhance comprehension and retention for many learners. Introducing new vocabulary items within meaningful contexts can be accomplished through a variety of strategies. Here are four possible strategies to consider implementing in your classroom.

HACK #1

Sentence builders: Formerly referred to as substitution tables, sentence builders have gained popularity in recent years due to the efforts of Dr Gianfranco Conti (Conti, 2020a), who employs them in his EPI (Extensive Processing Instruction) approach (Conti, 2020b), which is based on the notion that teaching language through chunks (e.g. polywords, collocation, sentence heads and frames) is much more effective than teaching isolated words as it is more economic in terms of cognitive load. It consists of instructional sequences and techniques focused on the development of communicative skills. A sentence builder involves organising words, phrases and clauses in a structured manner to convey thoughts, ideas or information effectively. These new lexical items are introduced via sentence builders and extensively practised across all four modalities to ensure their deep-rooted retention in long-term memory and to foster fluency development. For more information on this approach, visit the website https://gianfrancoconti.com/.

HACK #2

Parallel texts: This is an approach pioneered by Barry Smith about 20 years ago. It involves presenting a text in L1 on the left side with its translation into the L2 on the right side. The approach emphasises the importance of making the target language transparent for learners. It advocates for various strategies, including literal translation, font changes, numbered lines and extensive recycling of language. The goal is to build confidence and familiarity with the language while

13

focusing on pronunciation, syntax and vocabulary. The approach involves gradual removal of scaffolding to encourage independent learning. By promoting attention to detail and providing support tailored to individual needs, students develop agency, self-belief and independence. One of the advantages of parallel texts, particularly when the translation remains as accurate as possible, is that it fosters 'noticing', which supports not just development of the lexicon, but also grammar. Through consistent practice and attention to detail, students improve their reading, speaking and listening skills while developing effective learning habits. Barry does consultancy work in MFL and school culture. His contact details can be found in the Acknowledgements section.

1.	I like to go to the cinema.	J'aime aller au cinéma.	1.	I like to go to the cinema.	J'**me aller au cin*ma.
2.	I like to go to the cinema with my brother.	J'aime aller au cinéma avec mon frère.	2.	I like to go to the cinema with my brother.	J'**me aller au cin*ma avec mon fr*re.
3.	I like to go to the theatre with my father.	J'aime aller au théâtre avec mon père.	3.	I like to go to the theatre with my father.	J'**me aller au th**tre avec mon p*re.
4.	I like to go to the stadium with my grandfather.	J'aime aller au stade avec mon grand-père.	4.	I like to go to the stadium with my grandfather.	J'**me aller ** stade avec mon grand-p*re.
5.	I like to go to the park with my uncle.	J'aime aller au parc avec mon oncle.	5.	I like to go to the park with my uncle.	J'**me aller ** parc avec m*n oncle.
6.	I like to go to the garden public with my cousin.	J'aime aller au jardin public avec mon cousin.	6.	I like to go to the garden public with my cousin.	J'**me all*r ** jard*n p*blic avec m*n c**sin.

1.	I like to go to the cinema.	J' a a c. (AA)
2.	I like to go to the cinema with my brother.	J' a a c (AA) a m f. (AG)
3.	I like to go to the theatre with my father.	J' a a t (AA, AC) a m p. (AG)
4.	I like to go to the stadium with my grandfather.	J' a a s a m g-p. (AG)
5.	I like to go to the park with my uncle.	J' a a p a m o.
6.	I like to go to the garden public with my cousin.	J' a a j p a m c.

Est-ce que je suis sportif? Figure-toi, franchement, je ne vais pas te mentir, le sport, honnêtement, pour ne rien te cacher, ça ne m'intéresse pas trop. Tout simplement, ce n'est pas mon truc. En fin de compte, ma devise de vie, c'est, chacun ses goûts. Vivre et laisser vivre. Il faut de tout pour faire un monde. Comme on dit. Mais moi, je suis plutôt du genre, comment dire, moi, je préfère végéter devant la télé, manger de la pizza en buvant de la bière. Personne n'est parfait! On a tous les défauts! Mais, ce n'est pas la fin du monde non plus! Et toi? Tu dirais que tu es sportif ou non?	Est-ce q** je s**s sportif? Figure-t**, franchement, je ne v**s pas te mentir, le sport, honn*tement, p**r ne r**n te cacher, ça ne m'*ntéresse pas trop. T**t simplement, ce n'*st pas mon truc. En f*n de compte, ma devise de v**, c'*st, chacun ses g**ts. Vivre et l**sser vivre. Il f**t de t**t p**r f**re un monde. Comme *n d*t. M**s m**, je s**s plut*t du genre, comment d*re, m**, je pr*f*re v*g*ter devant la t*l*, manger d* l* pizza en b*vant de la b**re. Personne n'*st parf**t! On a t**s les d*f**ts! M**s, ce n'*st pas l* f*n d* m*nd* non plus! Et t**? Tu dir**s q** t* *s sport*f ** non?

Examples of Barry's parallel texts demonstrating different levels of scaffolding and challenge

HACK #3

Teaching via narratives (emails and letters): This approach to teaching new language shared by Hannah Pinkham (Myatt & Tomsett, 2021), was introduced in her previous school, and aimed to address students' struggles with understanding and applying grammar. The strategy involved reducing cognitive load by front-loading vocabulary and exposing students to varied tenses and grammatical structures in a high-challenge, low-threat manner via stories. Younger students learned practical vocabulary, and explicit grammar instruction was introduced in Year 9. This phased strategy helped students grasp vocabulary first, making grammar more accessible later.

The curriculum featured key phrases and structures within standard topics, incorporating narratives involving characters from different Hispanic countries to integrate cultural elements. For example, stories included characters from Madrid, Bolivia and Colombia, culminating in a shared trip in Year 8 that, at the time, aligned with students' real-life experiences. The teaching strategy emphasised listening first, using dramatic readings and gestures (similar to TPRS, see below) without showing the text initially. This was followed by a three-column approach to text analysis: target language, literal translation and idiomatic translation. Pronunciation and reading aloud were also prioritised.

HACK #4

Teaching Proficiency through Reading and Storytelling (TPRS): This is an approach created in the late 1980s by Blaine Ray (a Spanish teacher) – influenced by the work of Dr Stephen Krashen (Input Hypothesis) and Dr James Asher (Total Physical Response (TPR)) – that aims to immerse the language learner in repeated exposure to high-frequency, fully understandable language structures while collaboratively creating a class story.

The strategy has three steps:

- **Introducing new structures**: The teacher introduces the new language by selecting three to four high-frequency, target language (TL) structures as the foundation of the story. For a novice story, it might include the TL structures: there is/wants to/goes to/has (Printer, 2019). At this stage, meaning is established through TPR, which is the use of actions to mimic or direct students to the new structures, i.e. using gesturing. Once students show comprehension through their actions, the teacher introduces Personalised Questions. These are targeted questions about students' personal interests that incorporate the new structures.
- **Class storytelling**: In TPRS, the teacher begins with a plot of the story, however he or she does not simply narrate the story. Instead, they collaboratively construct the narrative with the students, prompting them to contribute details or characters and using questions to guide the narrative structure and allowing students to contribute, enhancing their engagement and understanding. The teacher reiterates the structures throughout the story and employs TPR again by having students act out parts of the narrative. This approach reinforces their learning and provides a motivating classroom environment.
- **Class reading**: The objective of this stage is to transition students from processing aural input to processing written input. In this phase, students are presented with different versions of their own story, as well as other similar stories with some altered details. The reading material solidifies students' understanding by placing the structures in a broader context, improving their comprehension and retention.

TPRS aims to create a stress-free and highly motivating learning environment, encouraging students to respond enthusiastically to statements. These responses might be phrases like 'ooh' or 'no way!'.

> Example of how you could build a story using TPRS (courtesy of Dr Liam Printer)
>
> **Teacher:** There is a man. He has a moustache. But it isn't an ordinary moustache. He has a pencil for a moustache!
>
> **Students:** Ooh ... no way!
>
> **Teacher:** Who is there?
>
> **Students:** A man!
>
> **Teacher:** Yes! There is a man. Does he have a beard?
>
> **Students:** No!
>
> **Teacher:** Exactly! He does not have a beard. He has a moustache. Does he have an ordinary moustache?
>
> **Students:** No! ...

Example of a text in Spanish: Beginner – *El bigote raro* – *Hay, tiene, va, está a* (courtesy of Dr Liam Printer)

> **Target structures**
>
> Hay
>
> Va a
>
> Quiere
>
> Tiene miedo de
>
> **El cuento de Brad Pitt y el bigote**
>
> Hay un chico. Se llama <u>Brad Pitt</u>. Está en <u>Starbucks en París</u>. Brad es muy muy muy guapo. Tiene <u>un unicornio, dos pingüinos y tres tortugas</u>. Tiene una amiga que se llama <u>Kim Kardashian</u>. Brad tiene otro amigo, pero es un secreto. El otro amigo se llama Mario. Mario es más guapo, más inteligente y más alto que Brad. Brad está celoso de Mario, pero no dice nada.
>
> Pero hay un problema. Brad tiene bigote en la forma de <u>lápiz</u>!! Brad no tiene barba. Brad no está contento. Está triste porque tiene bigote en la forma de lápiz. Quiere <u>un sacapuntas</u>. ¡Es obvio! Entonces, Brad va a <u>la casa de Kim Kardashian</u>.
>
> Le dice:
>
> – Hola Kim. ¿Cómo estás mi amiga? Tengo un problema. Quiero un sacapuntas porque tengo bigote en la forma de lápiz. Soy feo.

- Hola Brad. Tú no eres feo. ¡Tú eres guapo Brad! ¡A mí me gusta tu bigote! No es un problema. Eres muy muy muy muy muy guapo.
- Gracias Kim, pero quiero un sacapuntas. ¿Tú tienes un sacapuntas para mí?
- No. Lo siento Brad. No tengo sacapuntas para tí. – dice Kim.

Brad está triste. Entonces, Brad va a la casa de <u>George Clooney</u>. Brad quiere un sacapuntas. Brad va a la casa de George Clooney. Va a la casa <u>en tren</u>. El tren no es muy rápido. Brad está en el tren <u>dieciocho días, once horas y siete minutos</u>.

Brad dice a George:

- Hola George. Me llamo Brad. Tengo un problema. Quiero un sacapuntas porque tengo bigote en la forma de lápiz. Soy feo.
- Hola Brad. ¿Tú quieres un sacapuntas?
- Sí, ¿tú tienes un sacapuntas para mí? – dice Brad
- Yo tengo muchos sacapuntas, pero no tengo sacapuntas para tí. Lo siento. – dice George

Brad está triste. Entonces, Brad va al <u>supermercado</u>. El supermercado se llama '<u>El mundo de los sacapuntas</u>'. <u>Lady Gaga</u> trabaja en el supermercado.

Brad le dice:

- Hola. Me llamo Brad. Tengo un problema. Quiero un sacapuntas porque tengo bigote en la forma de lápiz. Soy feo.
- Hola Brad. ¿Tú quieres un sacapuntas? No eres feo.
- Sí, soy feo. ¿Tú tienes un sacapuntas para mí? – dice Brad
- No eres feo. Me gusta tu bigote. – dice Lady Gaga
- Yo quiero un sacapuntas por favor. – dice Brad

Lady Gaga le da un sacapuntas. Lady Gaga le dice:

- Brad. Tú no quieres el sacapuntas. Eres perfecto. Tú tienes bigote en la forma de lápiz. Es increíble ... Eh ... ¿quieres ir al cine conmigo?
- ¿contigo? – dice Brad
- Sí, conmigo. – dice Lady Gaga

Brad non dice nada. Brad toma el sacapuntas y corre. Lady Gaga está triste.

Benefits

Understanding TPRS is straightforward and immensely beneficial. This strategy not only improves language comprehension but also makes learning interactive, motivating and engaging. Implementing TPRS, especially for young learners, will effectively expand their language skills and foster a deeper interest in the subject.

Conclusion

While some schools may still rely on single-word instruction for teaching new languages, incorporating a variety of vocabulary instruction approaches, such as sentence builders, knowledge organisers, parallel texts, narratives and TPRS, each advocating for extensive practice, can significantly enhance the effectiveness, memorability and retention of language learning. These diverse approaches cater to different learners and classroom settings by providing multiple entry points and scaffolding opportunities, as well as chances to recycle and revisit vocabulary and language structures. This engagement reduces cognitive load and facilitates long-term retention of language skills. Furthermore, these strategies empower learners to use their language knowledge communicatively, promoting both language acquisition and fluency. Therefore, adopting a range of teaching strategies tailored to specific classroom and school contexts not only boosts engagement but also ensures meaningful learning outcomes in language education.

CHAPTER 3
TEACHING GRAMMAR

In Malachi's Year 10 German class, the learning objective of the lesson is: 'Expressing opinions and justifying them using a variety of conjunctions'. Considering that many students in the class aim for grades 7 or higher in their final examinations, it might seem straightforward. However, it is not quite that simple.

You see, Malachi is not new to the world of German grammar. He has been navigating the twists and turns of the language since Year 7. He has encountered sentences with 'und', 'aber', 'oder', 'denn', 'weil' and 'dass' before, and he knows they are important for connecting ideas and giving reasons. But here is the catch: while Malachi's previous teachers introduced him to these conjunctions, they never really explained the mechanics of this grammar concept in depth, particularly regarding how certain conjunctions can impact the word order in the sentence. Sure, Malachi knows that sometimes the verb has to move to the end in German sentences. He has seen it happen plenty of times in different concepts. But why does it happen? And when should this happen? These are the questions that keep swirling around in Malachi's mind as he sits in his German class, feeling utterly confused.

Miss Murray, his current teacher, is fantastic and very passionate about German, and genuinely cares about her students' success. She is introducing conjunctions like 'wenn', 'als' and 'obwohl', placing them at the beginning of sentences while mentioning something about 'verb comma verb rule', and the concept of word order is becoming even more confusing to Malachi! Recognising the need for immediate action, Miss Murray decides to tackle the issue head-on by explicitly teaching the grammar concept of the complexities of German word order, breaking it down into chunks and modelling it directly, checking students' understanding at each stage.

This case study highlights an interesting issue. Malachi has never been explicitly taught the difference between coordinating and subordinating conjunctions. In German, this is a complex grammatical concept, and a step-by-step teaching approach could have been beneficial. An initial explicit explanation of the rule early on during his language learning journey, perhaps in Year 7 when introducing the subordinating conjunction '*weil*', would have been particularly helpful.

Grammar is generally defined as a set of rules that enables us to construct sentences. Research on the effectiveness of implicit and explicit teaching of grammar in MFL often varies in findings and methodologies. Both approaches have their advantages and disadvantages, and their effectiveness can depend on a range of factors such as learners' age, proficiency level and the specific grammatical feature being taught.

Implicit versus explicit approaches to grammar teaching

Implicit teaching, referred to as incidental or inductive, prioritises **meaning**.

Advantages:

- It mimics natural language acquisition, where learners pick up grammar through CI, exposure and practice. Lexicogrammar is a level of linguistic structure where lexis (vocabulary) and grammar or syntax combine into one and are not seen as independent but rather mutually dependent, with one level interfacing with the other (Sardinha, 2019). This is also the approach observed in initial stages of Conti's EPI (Conti, 2018).
- It promotes communicative competence as learners focus on using the language rather than analysing its structure.
- It can be more engaging and enjoyable for learners.

Disadvantages:

- It may not provide sufficient explanations for learners who prefer explicit instruction.
- Some grammatical features may not be easily acquired implicitly, especially more complex or abstract ones.
- Progress might be slower compared to explicit instruction, especially for certain grammar points, and cause issues in further studies, i.e. in progression at A-level.

In contrast, **explicit** teaching, known as the deductive or intentional approach, emphasises the mastery of **forms**.

Advantages:

- It is preplanned and so provides clear explanations of grammatical rules.
- It helps learners to understand the structure of the language systematically.
- It is suitable for learners who prefer structured learning environments.

Disadvantages:

- It may be less engaging for some learners as grammar is taught in isolation.

- Learners might focus more on memorisation – mechanical drills – rather than practical application.
- It can be overwhelming if too much information is presented at once.

There is often a disparity between the grammar that learners comprehend in reading or listening and the grammar they can produce accurately in speech or writing. Therefore, learners need extensive practice in both modalities (oral and written) and both modes (comprehension and production). Research findings on the effectiveness of these approaches vary. Some studies suggest that explicit instruction can be beneficial (Kasprowicz & Marsden, 2018; Avery et al., 2019; Müller et al., 2018) and is more effective for certain aspects of grammar, such as irregular verb conjugations or complex sentence structures, while implicit instruction may be more effective for developing fluency and natural language use (Communicative Language Teaching (CLT), Zhang, 2023). Other studies indicate that a combination of both approaches, known as a 'balanced' approach, may yield the best results, catering to different learning preferences.

Additionally, factors such as classroom context, teacher expertise, instructional materials and learner motivation can influence the effectiveness of both implicit and explicit teaching methods. Therefore, it is essential for language teachers to consider these factors when designing instructional approaches and curriculum.

What are the concerns when teaching grammar concepts explicitly?

Potential problems with explicit instruction:

- providing too much information at once, such as entire verb paradigms
- moving on too quickly from explanation to production
- practising the concept in isolation with just mechanical drills, causing learners to struggle with transferring the knowledge to production
- insufficient active practice to link the concept to meaning in input.

Frequently, these issues arise in the way grammar is portrayed and practised across many textbooks.

Chapter 3 TEACHING GRAMMAR

Which grammar concepts do our students find challenging, and how can we address these difficulties when using an explicit teaching approach?

HACK #1

The burger: Teaching the past perfect tense in German poses a consistent challenge, primarily due to the complexities of word order in the language. To help my students, I use a visual aid – called the 'burger' – a strategy I learned during my PGCE training about 20 years ago, to explain the concept explicitly. Initially, I introduce the past perfect tense in English, discussing regular past participles and their construction. Then, I transition to German, guiding students through the process of forming regular past participles. Once they grasp this, we use the 'burger' analogy to illustrate sentence construction and word order. I begin with the auxiliary verb '*haben*' in the first person singular. We extensively practise this structure before advancing to irregular verbs, the auxiliary verb '*sein*', and addressing sentences involving other 'people'. To solidify comprehension, we continually revisit and space our practice in different contexts, ensuring thorough reinforcement of this grammatical concept through all modes and modalities.

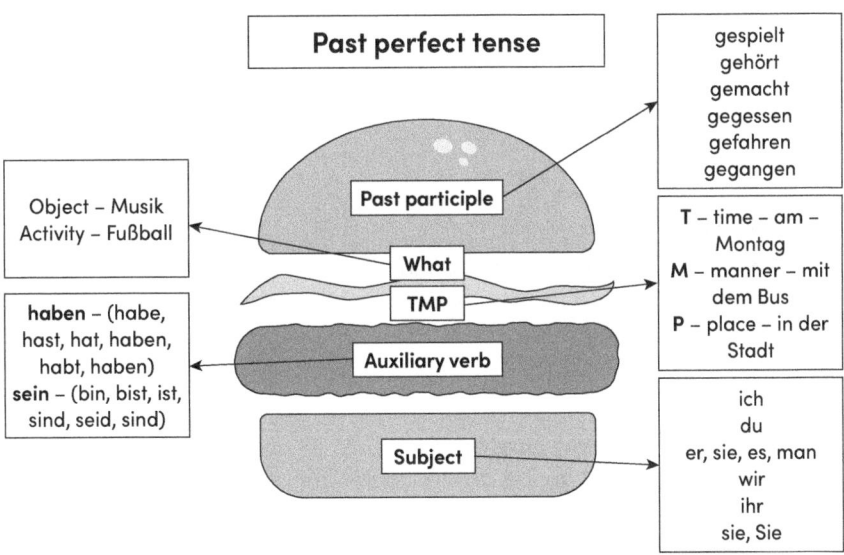

The 'burger'

HACK #2

'Verb booters': In German, certain conjunctions like *'weil'*, *'dass'*, *'obwohl'*, *'wenn'* and *'als'* influence the word order in sentences, particularly the placement of the verb. I refer to these conjunctions as 'verb booters' because they effectively 'boot' the verb to the end of the sentence. To aid my learners in grasping this challenging concept, I have introduced this visual aid. However, to ensure this understanding sticks in long-term memory, it is crucial to offer ample opportunities for meaningful input and output, both receptively and productively, through consistent and spaced practice.

WEIL/because

When using 'WEIL' you must always boot the verb to the end of the sentence!!

Ich lerne gern Geschichte.
Es ist interessant.

Ich lerne gern Geschichte, **weil** es interessant **ist**.

weil – a 'verb booter'

Ser y estar

Teaching the distinction between *ser* and *estar* to students can be challenging, as English only has one verb, 'to be', while Spanish uses two. Here's a structured approach to help students grasp this difference effectively.

 HACK #3

Introduce the concepts with simple examples: Begin by explaining that *ser* and *estar* are both used for 'to be', but that each has a different purpose. *Ser* is for permanent characteristics, identity, time and origin, while *estar* is for temporary states, locations and emotions. Use visuals, like charts, to reinforce these categories.

🔒 HACK #4

Create mnemonics for memory aid: Use mnemonics such as 'DOCTOR' (Description, Occupation, Characteristics, Time, Origin and Relationships) for *ser*, and 'PLACE' (Position, Location, Action, Condition and Emotion) for *estar*. These acronyms help students remember when to use each verb.

DOCTOR vs PLACE	
Ser = DOCTOR	*Estar* = PLACE
D – descriptions	P – place
O – occupations	L – location
C – characteristics	A – actions in progress
T – time	C – conditions/states
O – origin	E – emotions/symptoms
R – relationships	

🔒 MORE HACKS TO TEACH *SER* AND *ESTAR*

- **Incorporate role play and real-life scenarios**: Create sentences that students can use in role-play exercises. For example, '*Soy profesor*' ('I am a teacher') vs '*Estoy cansado*' ('I am tired'). Real-life situations make the differences between *ser* and *estar* more relatable.
- **Use comparative exercises**: Provide pairs of sentences to show how meaning changes with each verb. For example, '*Él es listo*' ('He is smart') vs '*Él está listo*' ('He is ready'). This helps students see how *ser* and *estar* shape meaning in different ways.
- **Practice through interactive games**: Use games, such as sentence-matching activities, where students choose between *ser* and *estar* based on context. This reinforces usage in a fun and memorable way.
- Remember, always follow the golden rule: for what you feel and where you are, always use the verb *ESTAR*!

The *passé composé*

Similarly, teaching the passé composé to students can be simplified by focusing on its structure, usage and comparisons with English. Here are some approaches to introduce the concept effectively.

HACK #5

Introduce the concept and structure: Begin by explaining that *passé composé* is used for past actions, similar to 'I have done' or 'I did' in English. Break down the structure into two parts: an auxiliary verb (*avoir* or *être*) and the past participle. Use examples like '*J'ai mangé*' ('I ate') and '*Je suis allé*' ('I went') to show the form in practice.

 HACK #6

Focus on avoir before être: Start with *avoir* verbs, as they are more common. Practise with regular -er, -ir and -re verbs to reinforce regular conjugation patterns (e.g. *manger* → *mangé*). Once students feel comfortable, introduce *être* verbs and the mnemonic 'DR & MRS VANDERTRAMP' to help remember verbs that require *être*.

 MORE HACKS TO SUPPORT THE *PASSÉ COMPOSE*

- **Use timelines and visual aids**: To clarify that *passé composé* is used for completed actions, create timelines that contrast it with the *imparfait*, showing that *passé composé* refers to actions with a clear start and end in the past. Visuals can reinforce this concept.
- **Interactive drills and storytelling**: Use short, storytelling exercises where students create sentences using *passé composé*. For example, give them prompts like 'Yesterday, I ...' and encourage them to build sentences that link actions, using the correct auxiliary and past participle.
- **Comparative translation practice**: Give sentences in English (e.g. 'I watched a movie yesterday.') and have students translate them, focusing on when and how to use *passé composé* accurately. This will help them relate the structure and purpose to English past tenses.

By breaking down the structure, focusing on *avoir* verbs first, using visual aids, practising interactively and providing comparative examples, students can develop a solid grasp of the *passé composé*.

Conclusion

These language hacks can offer powerful tools for tackling common grammar challenges in German, Spanish and French. By using structured techniques, students can build a deeper grasp of each concept. Combined, these hacks make complex grammar topics more approachable and enhance retention through consistent practice, visualisation and interactive engagement.

CHAPTER 4
INCORPORATING CULTURE

Incorporating culture into MFL teaching is not only about developing students' linguistic skills but also about fostering a deeper understanding of the people and contexts where the target language is spoken. It aims to open minds and open doors to the wider world around students, thereby fostering aspirations beyond the classroom. Engaging students with the cultural elements of a language creates a richer learning experience, broadens their global awareness, develops sensitivity and increases their motivation to learn. This cultural awareness enhances and connects language learning to real-life situations.

The importance of culture in language learning

Language and culture are inseparable. Culture shapes the way people speak, interpret meaning and interact. By exposing students to the traditions, customs and social norms of target-language communities, teachers help them grasp the nuances of communication that go beyond vocabulary and grammar. Incorporating culture into MFL classes leads to a more-holistic learning process, enabling students to engage with the language authentically.

Many learners might find it difficult to understand the relevance of learning a foreign language, particularly if they do not see an immediate application to their lives. Culture can bridge this gap by sparking curiosity and making the language more relatable and tangible. For example, exploring French cuisine, Spanish art, German composers or Chinese festivals provides context for vocabulary and grammar while igniting students' interest in the rich cultural heritage of the world around us.

However, the infusion of cultural elements into the curriculum must be intentional and systematic. Rather than simply adding 'fun facts' about different countries, teachers should seek to embed culture into lessons in meaningful ways that tie into language goals. A great example of this is the European Days of Languages, celebrated by many school communities in the month of September. This celebration offers students the opportunity to improve language skills while having a greater appreciation for the linguistic diversity of Europe and beyond. Here, we explore a mere snippet of how we can incorporate cultural opportunities in the classroom.

HACK #1

Virtual visits: One way to bring culture to life is by taking students on virtual visits. Many museums, historical sites and cultural landmarks around the world offer free online tours. We can create a lesson around visiting the Alhambra in Spain, the Louvre in Paris, the castle Neuschwanstein in Germany or Kandinsky's kaleidoscope where students explore art, architecture, history and more while practising the relevant vocabulary. These immersive experiences create a strong connection between language and culture, making learning more relevant, meaningful and memorable.

 HACK #2

Celebrate cultural events: Just like our celebration of the European Day of Languages, dedicating time to celebrate cultural events, and embedding them in the curriculum, allows students to participate in traditions and customs from the target culture. Whether it is cooking a traditional meal, learning about '*El día de los muertos*' in Spanish class, Fasching / Karneval in German or researching Bastille Day in French, these activities make language learning enjoyable and practical. It also helps students recognise the cultural values tied to these holidays, encouraging them to engage with the language beyond the classroom.

 HACK #3

Incorporate authentic materials: Using authentic materials – including music, films, podcasts and news articles – helps students experience how native speakers use the language in real-life contexts. We can dedicate time to listening to popular music or watching short clips from local news channels. Discussing cultural themes, such as family traditions or social issues, enhances students' listening skills and cultural understanding.

 HACK #4

Cultural pen pals: A strategy that has been around for decades and is still relevant. Establishing connections with students and schools in the target country through email exchanges or video calls offers a direct way for students to experience another culture. This interaction encourages authentic communication and provides a window into the daily lives of students in other countries. Through these exchanges, students improve their writing and comprehension skills while developing intercultural awareness. There are many platforms or organisations like the British Council or the Global Alliance that can support this sort of work.

HACK #5

Role-play scenarios: Bringing cultural role-play scenarios into the classroom gives students an opportunity to practise language skills while navigating cultural norms. For example, we can stage situations like ordering food in a French café or participating in a German Sunday breakfast. These activities help students apply language to real-world situations and understand the cultural expectations around them.

Conclusion

Incorporating culture into the MFL classroom is essential for developing students into not only proficient linguists but also more-culturally-aware individuals. By blending language instruction with authentic cultural experiences, we can create a dynamic learning environment where curiosity thrives, and students feel more connected to the language they are learning.

SECTION 2: THE FOUR LANGUAGE SKILLS

In MFL education, proficiency in the four language skills – listening, speaking, reading and writing – is paramount to achieving communicative competence and linguistic fluency. Each of these skills plays a unique and complementary role in facilitating effective communication and language acquisition.

Listening skills enable learners to understand spoken language, whether in face-to-face interactions, audio recordings or multimedia resources. By refining their listening abilities, students develop the capacity to understand a wide range of accents, dialects and speech patterns, thereby enhancing their communicative competence in real-world contexts.

Similarly, **speaking skills** empower learners to express themselves fluently and accurately in the target language. Through speaking activities, such as conversations, role plays and presentations, students can gain confidence in articulating their thoughts, opinions and ideas. Speaking practice not only enhances students' oral proficiency but also fosters interactive communication skills, enabling them to engage in meaningful conversations and exchanges with native speakers and peers.

Reading skills are equally vital in MFL education, providing learners with access to a wealth of authentic texts, literature and cultural resources. Skilled readers can comprehend written language, extract key information and infer meaning from context. Reading proficiency enhances students' vocabulary acquisition, comprehension skills and cultural literacy, enriching their understanding of the target language and its cultural nuances.

Finally, **writing skills** enable learners to express themselves effectively through written communication. Whether crafting essays, emails or creative compositions, skilled writers demonstrate mastery of grammar, vocabulary and discourse conventions. Writing practice encourages students to articulate their thoughts with clarity and precision, fostering creativity and self-expression in the target language.

Listening
CHAPTER 5
DECODING AND PARSING SKILLS

Listening comprehension is one of the most challenging skills for foreign language learners, frequently causing anxiety (Graham, 2017), yet it plays a crucial role in developing overall language proficiency. The process of understanding spoken language in real time is far more complex than simply hearing and recognising words. It involves decoding the sounds of the language, parsing its grammatical structure and using contextual clues to infer meaning – all while operating within the narrow time window of just two seconds per sentence. In this highly demanding cognitive task, students often fall behind native speakers and struggle to retain information as incoming speech continuously replaces previous input.

The role of decoding in listening comprehension

Decoding is the ability to recognise and interpret sounds in a spoken language. This skill is especially important because students frequently struggle with the gap between written and spoken language. While they may easily recognise words in their written form, they often fail to understand these same words when spoken by native speakers, who may articulate them more quickly, blend sounds or use contractions and informal speech, making it hard for students to recognise familiar words when spoken aloud.

For example, a French learner might understand the word *'beaucoup'* in writing but fail to recognise it when it is spoken as /bo-ku/, with sounds blended and reduced. Similarly, English learners might struggle with connected speech where phrases like *'What are you going to do?'* become *'Whatcha gonna do?'*. These phonological shifts create a barrier to comprehension for learners who rely heavily on written forms.

Developing decoding skills is essential for overcoming this barrier. Listening exercises that focus on recognising silent letters, identifying phoneme blends and distinguishing between similar sounds (e.g. minimal pairs) can help students become more attuned to the nuances of native speech.

HACK #1

Phoneme discrimination: One foundational decoding activity involves phoneme discrimination, where students listen to minimal pairs (words that differ by only one sound) and identify which words they hear. This helps them tune their ears to the subtle differences between sounds in the target language. See examples in Chapter 1.

Another effective strategy is to have students listen to sentences read aloud by the teacher and highlight the letters or sounds that are silent or altered in speech. This practice increases awareness of how pronunciation deviates from the written form, helping students map sounds more accurately to the words they know.

HACK #2

Spot the silent letter: Students are provided with a list of sentences, like the one below, and listen to the teacher reading them aloud. Their task is to highlight the letters that are not pronounced by the teacher, as these letters are silent in the target language.

> Example:
>
> *Elle parle souvent aux voisins pendant l'après-midi.*
>
> In this sentence, students would highlight silent letters such as the second '*e*' in '*Elle*', the '*e*' in '*parle*', the '*t*' in '*souvent*', the '*x*' in '*aux*' and the '*t*' in '*pendant*'.

HACK #3

Spot the mistake: Students are given a list of words in a series. The teacher will pronounce each word, but in every series, one word is pronounced incorrectly. The students' task is to identify the mistake in pronunciation. They can do this by writing it on a mini whiteboard or by highlighting it on a handout.

> Example:
>
> Series of words: '*cama*', '*casa*', '*cera*', '*cena*'. The teacher pronounces them as: '*cama*' (correct), '*casa*' (correct), '*cara*' (incorrect, should be '*cera*'), '*cena*' (correct). Students should identify that '*cera*' was mispronounced.

Other activities could include gap-fills (scaffolded in the first instance via multiple choice), break the flow of the speech, rhyming pairs activities, etc.

Parsing as a key to sentence-level understanding

While decoding focuses on individual sounds and words, **parsing** is the skill of breaking down a sentence into its grammatical components to understand its meaning. This involves identifying the subject, verb, objects and modifiers within a sentence and understanding their relationships. Parsing is particularly important as students progress to more advanced stages of language learning, where they encounter complex sentence structures and need to navigate unfamiliar syntax.

For example, in languages like Spanish, Italian or French, students need to recognise the difference between verb conjugations and how they change according to subject and tense. In German, students need to recognise the difference between three genders, and understand cases and how they affect adjectives and determiners. They must also pay attention to verb placement to parse sentences accurately in German. In English, students may need to recognise phrasal verbs or distinguish between homophones based on context. Parsing becomes more challenging when dealing with fast speech or unfamiliar accents, as students must process the language in real time. Without strong parsing skills, students may understand individual words but fail to grasp the meaning of a sentence as a whole.

Teaching parsing skills requires explicit teaching of grammar and sentence structure. Activities such as sentence diagrams (puzzles), where students visually break down the components of a sentence, help clarify how words function together.

 HACK #4

Sentence puzzles: Give students a set of sentences where the words are scrambled and out of their correct order. The task is for the students to rearrange the words to form grammatically correct sentences. Providing students with a table labelled with different lexical categories (such as noun, verb, adjective, etc.) or grammatical relationships (such as subject, object, etc.) can make it easier for them to unscramble sentences. Here is how you can structure this activity using tables for different languages.

Examples:
Spanish: Scrambled sentence: *'el parque corriendo perro está en el.'*
Correct sentence: *'El perro está corriendo en el parque.'*
German: Scrambled sentence: *'das Buch seinem liest in er Zimmer.'*
Correct sentence: *'Er liest das Buch in seinem Zimmer.'*
French: Scrambled sentence: *'à maison elle va la.'*
Correct sentence: *'Elle va à la maison.'*

Subject	Verb	Preposition	Article	Object
Elle	va	à	la	maison

HACK #5

Listening for specific words or structures: In this activity, students focus on identifying specific grammatical structures or vocabulary in an audio passage. This hones their ability to decode the linguistic elements of spoken language while processing meaning.

 Listen for specific grammar point and make a tally in the table

present tense	past perfect tense	future tense	past imperfect	opinions	modal verbs

Example activity

Additionally, translation exercises can reinforce parsing skills, as students need to understand both the syntactic structure of the target language and their native language to produce accurate translations.

Conclusion

Decoding and parsing skills are important strategies for developing listening comprehension in MFL teaching. Together, these skills empower students to grasp complex linguistic patterns, understand sentence meaning and improve fluency in both written and spoken language.

By participating in the activities outlined above, students practise deconstructing language into its individual components, improving their ability to process information more effectively. Building these skills is important for mastering grammar, syntax and effective communication in any language.

CHAPTER 6
PREDICTION SKILLS AND INFERENCES

As discussed in the previous chapter, successful listening comprehension in a foreign language is not a passive activity but requires active involvement through various strategies. In this chapter, we will focus on prediction skills and making inferences. By encouraging students to anticipate content and analyse linguistic input, we, as language teachers, can help them navigate the complexities of listening in a new language.

Predicting can serve as an effective icebreaker by prompting students to use contextual clues and prior knowledge to anticipate what a speaker might say next. This strategy can help students prepare for the cognitive and linguistic challenges of listening, reduce anxiety and enhance their ability to derive meaning from spoken language. Predicting also encourages an active-listening approach, engaging students mentally before they even hear the target language. It involves using knowledge of the subject, grammar, vocabulary and cultural context to make educated guesses about the content. Teaching students to make informed guesses based on context has produced positive results in several research studies (Nassaji, 2003).

Why is predicting useful?

- **It engages students**: Predicting activates students' background knowledge, leading to deeper engagement with the material.
- **It builds confidence**: The ability to guess or predict certain elements gives students more confidence, especially in the early stages of language learning when listening can feel overwhelming.
- **It prepares for unknown vocabulary**: Students can handle unfamiliar words better if they have already made predictions about the general content.
- **It mimics real-life communication**: In everyday conversations, listeners often anticipate what the speaker will say next, using tone, gestures or contextual clues. Using predicting skills in the classroom better prepares students for authentic interactions.

Activities to develop predictive skills

HACK #1

Predicting from titles and images: A great way to develop predictive skills is through pre-listening activities that ask students to speculate about the content based on non-verbal cues. For example, before playing an audio recording or video, the teacher can show a title or image related to the material and ask students to predict what they might hear.

> Example activity
> The teacher shows a picture of a café or restaurant and asks students, 'What kind of conversation do you think will happen in this setting? What vocabulary might you expect to hear? Guess what comes next?' After generating predictions, the teacher plays the conversation, and students check their guesses against the actual content. You could then scaffold the activity by giving students a handout with the transcript split across a mosaic (jigsaw) puzzle.

HACK #2

Gap-fill listening exercises: Gap-fill exercises encourage predicting by requiring students to guess missing words before hearing the full audio. Students are given a transcript with blanks in key areas and must predict the missing words based on the surrounding context, engaging them with the material before listening.

Example activity

In a dialogue between two friends planning a weekend trip, blanks are left where time expressions or place names would appear. Students predict these based on the situation, then listen to the audio and fill in the gaps.

Anna: Hey Lukas! Hast du schon Pläne für das _____ (1)?

Lukas: Hallo Anna! Noch nicht. Ich überlege, ob ich nach _____ (2) oder _____ (3) fahren soll. Was hast du vor?

Anna: Ich habe daran gedacht, nach _____ (4) zu fahren. Das Wetter wird gut, und es ist nicht zu weit.

Lukas: Gute Idee! Wir könnten am Samstag um _____ (5) losfahren. Was denkst du?

Anna: Klingt gut! Aber ich muss spätestens am Sonntag um _____ (6) zurück sein, ich habe ein Abendessen mit meiner Familie.

Lukas: Kein Problem. Wir könnten am Sonntag gegen _____ (7) zurückkommen.

Berlin	10 Uhr	Wochenende	20 Uhr	Hamburg	18 Uhr	die Berge

 HACK #3

Sequencing events: Another common prediction activity is to give students a set of events or statements in random order. Before listening, students predict the correct sequence of events and then verify their predictions during or after the listening task.

Setting it up:

- **Pre-listening prediction**: Before listening, students should predict the correct order of events by arranging them based on what they think makes sense.
- **Listening**: Play the audio or read the text aloud. Students should listen attentively to verify whether their predictions match the sequence in the text.
- **Post-listening verification**: After listening, review the correct sequence with students, discussing any differences and noting key words that helped them understand the order of events.

> Example: Suggested events (to be given to students in random order):
> 1. Marta desayuna tostada y jugo de naranja.
> 2. Marta juega al fútbol en el recreo.
> 3. Marta se da cuenta de que olvidó su cuaderno de matemáticas.
> 4. Marta se despierta a las seis de la mañana.
> 5. Marta regresa a casa cansada pero contenta.
> 6. Marta cena con su familia y se va a dormir.
> 7. La amiga de Marta, Laura, le presta un cuaderno.
>
> The complete text for students to compare their predictions:
>
> **Hoy fue un día muy ocupado para Marta.** *Primero, se despertó a las seis de la mañana y tomó una ducha rápida. Después, se vistió y se preparó el desayuno, que consistió en una tostada y un jugo de naranja. Al terminar de desayunar, salió de casa y fue a la escuela. Al llegar, se dio cuenta de que había olvidado su cuaderno de matemáticas, ¡qué desastre! Afortunadamente, su amiga Laura le prestó uno. Más tarde, durante el recreo, Marta y sus amigos jugaron al fútbol en el patio. Al final del día, regresó a casa cansada pero contenta. Finalmente, cenó con su familia y se fue a dormir temprano para descansar.*

This activity encourages students to actively engage with the text and practise sequencing and comprehension.

> Example GCSE activity:
>
> Students receive sentences summarising different parts of a story or conversation, arranged in a random order or cut up. They predict the correct sequence, then listen to confirm whether their predictions were accurate.

Inferences: Going beyond the literal meaning

While predicting is about anticipating what will be said, inference-making involves interpreting meaning that is not explicitly stated, such as understanding a speaker's intention, tone or implied meaning. This skill is often tested in high-stakes listening exams and is one that students typically find most challenging.

Inferences are crucial to communication, allowing listeners to grasp implied meanings, cultural references or figurative language. For example, in foreign language learning, students may not understand every word, but they can still grasp the general meaning by interpreting context, tone and non-literal language. Inference-making is especially important for understanding idiomatic expressions or cultural references, such as when a French speaker says, '*Il pleut des cordes*' (literal meaning: 'It's raining ropes'), students must infer that it means 'It's raining heavily'.

HACK #4

Listening for context clues: Play an audio recording featuring some unfamiliar vocabulary. Encourage students to use context clues from the surrounding words to infer the meanings of these new words. Discuss as a class. For students who might need extra support, consider providing a transcript as a scaffolding tool. After the activity, prompt students with some metacognitive questions such as: 'What clues helped you guess the meaning of this word?' or 'Can you think of a synonym or antonym based on the context?'.

> Example:
> In a recoding where one of the speakers is describing a busy marketplace, ask students: 'What do you think "buzzing with energy" means in this context?'.

HACK #5

Summarising: After listening to an audio recording, ask students to summarise the main points while inferring any underlying themes or messages and then discuss their notes as a class. For students who might need extra support, consider providing a transcript or use the 'think-pair-share' strategy as a scaffolding tool. After the activity, prompt students with some metacognitive questions such as: 'What is the main idea of what you heard, and what do you think the speaker feels about it?' or 'What ideas or themes did you notice in the listening task, and how did you figure them out?'.

Conclusion

Developing predictive skills and the ability to make inferences can significantly boost students' listening comprehension and engagement with spoken language. By encouraging and teaching students to anticipate outcomes and read between the lines, we can equip them with essential tools to understand not just what is said explicitly, but also the underlying meanings and emotions. These skills promote critical thinking, enabling students to draw connections, make informed guesses and deepen their overall understanding. As students practise these strategies, they become more-confident listeners and more-skilled communicators who can, as a result, better navigate more complex narratives and conversations in various contexts.

Speaking
CHAPTER 7
ROLE PLAY

Role play is a powerful tool in MFL teaching. It simply transforms the classroom into a place where students practise their speaking in real-life situations, allowing them the opportunity to use their vocabulary, grammar and pronunciation in meaningful conversations. By simulating everyday situations, role play encourages students to use the target language authentically, enhancing fluency and confidence. Furthermore, role playing as a pedagogic activity has some other more important advantages regarding the development of social and cultural competence in the process of negotiating different norms of communication within the given target culture.

One of the biggest challenges in language learning is moving from passive understanding to active use. Role play provides a safe environment where students can experiment with the language, make mistakes and learn from them without the pressure of real-world consequences. Such active use of language consolidates grammatical structures and vocabulary, and makes retrieval and use of them far easier in conversation.

Additionally, role play integrates culture with language learning. Students are exposed to the social cues, gestures and formalities of the target culture, allowing them to practise not just what to say but how to say it appropriately. For example, students learning French might practise ordering food at a café, where they also learn to navigate the cultural nuances of politeness and greetings.

 HACK #1

Scaffold the activity with sentence starters and key phrases: For many students, role plays present a challenge simply because of not knowing how to initiate or keep a conversation going. They become stuck as soon as they hear a phrase they do not understand fully and often lack the resilience to use strategies like common sense and the understanding of cognates to decipher meaning. We can provide scaffolding by giving students sentence starters and key phrases relevant to the role-play scenario. For example, if the students are in a restaurant dialogue, phrases such as 'I would like …' or 'Could you recommend …?' give them a structured way to begin their conversations. Over time, students will gain confidence and rely less on these prompts.

HACK #2

Use role-play cards to create realistic scenarios: Providing students with role-play cards that outline different scenarios can make the activity more structured and engaging. For example, one student could play the role of a shopkeeper while the other is a customer. Each card might include the student's role, objectives and some suggested phrases. The students become deeply involved in what they are doing because they are aware of their specific roles and have to think over how to achieve their aims with the use of target language. Role-play cards can be adapted to the proficiency level of the students, ensuring all learners feel challenged but not overwhelmed.

HACK #3

Incorporate props and visuals: Using props or visual aids can bring role plays to life and make the language more tangible. For example, for a role-play scenario set in a market, we might provide students with play money or even food items. Other visuals, such as restaurant menus or travel brochures, may help guide the conversation toward real situations. This multisensory approach engages students and makes the language-learning process more enjoyable and memorable.

HACK #4

Encourage group and peer feedback: Group- or peer-feedback sessions provide a good opportunity for students to reflect on and improve their performance after a role-play activity. We can encourage students to provide constructive feedback to their peers, focusing on both strengths and areas for improvement. This process helps students develop self-awareness and identify gaps in their language use. Additionally, feedback sessions give teachers an opportunity to address common mistakes or reinforce key language points for the whole class. In some classes, students may work in trios, with two students engaging in conversation and one observing, providing useful and supportive prompts and feedback.

HACK #5

Swap roles to increase language exposure: To ensure all students get the most out of role-play activities, it's important to rotate roles. For example, if students are practising a hotel scenario, have each student play the role of both the employee and the guest. This allows them to practise a wider range of vocabulary and grammar structures. Rotating roles also keeps the activity dynamic and engaging, as students are exposed to different perspectives and language functions, as well as finding themselves in situations whereby they are very much out of their comfort zones. Supported adequately, this can increase confidence and promote meaningful application of speaking skills.

Conclusion

Role play can be a motivating and interactive way to help students develop their speaking skills in MFL. By simulating real-world scenarios, students gain practical experience in using the target language, building both confidence and fluency. With thoughtful planning and the use of scaffolding, props, feedback and role rotation, we can create an engaging and supportive environment, minimising the perceived threat, where students thrive and enjoy their language-learning journey.

CHAPTER 8
PHOTO CARD

The photo-card activity is a staple in MFL teaching, particularly when preparing students for speaking assessments. The activity encourages students to think critically about what they see, and respond with appropriate vocabulary, grammar and cultural knowledge. This versatile speaking task helps develop descriptive language skills, expand vocabulary and improve fluency. It also mimics real-life scenarios whereby visual stimuli activate spontaneous conversation, such as discussing travel experiences or describing an event.

Under the new format, students are given a photo card containing two photos from one of the three themes during their supervised preparation time immediately before the test. This preparation period allows them to plan their response to the first compulsory question, which focuses on the content of the two photos. During this time, students may make written notes, which they are permitted to use during the task. The task is divided into two key parts: the response to the content of the photos and the unprepared conversation that follows.

When describing the photos, students must mention at least one thing about each photo. While coverage of the two images does not have to be equal, this ensures that both are addressed. Importantly, any relevant content mentioned in this section will be credited, even if it falls outside the prescribed theme of the card.

The second part is the unprepared conversation. This conversation draws on the theme specified on the candidate's card but may cover any of the three topics within that theme. This allows students to demonstrate their ability to produce more personalised responses and to apply their language knowledge flexibly in real time.

One of the biggest challenges students face in MFL is to speak spontaneously as well as remembering to use the most basic tools to respond to this activity. The photo-card activity presents a visual stimulus, which serves as a springboard for speaking. It encourages students to move beyond memorised phrases and to apply language skills to describe what they see. This task also strengthens cultural awareness, as the photos used can depict elements from the target culture, sparking discussions that incorporate both language and cultural context.

The photo-card activity helps students prepare for oral exams by practising in class and also under timed conditions. It develops their ability to predict questions and to use language more flexibly in answering unpredictable questions. By integrating this into classroom activities on a regular basis, students can build the confidence needed to speak on a range of topics.

HACK #1

The PALM(A) method continues to be a reliable framework. When working with two photos, students can describe each one briefly using PALM(A):

- **P** – People: Who can the students see?
- **A** – Action: What is happening? What are the people doing?
- **L** – Location: Where is the picture set?
- **M** – Mood: How do the people/items in the photo seem?

In some classrooms, we opt to add additional details (A), such as the weather, to further develop descriptions and explanations, meaning PALM becomes PALMA.

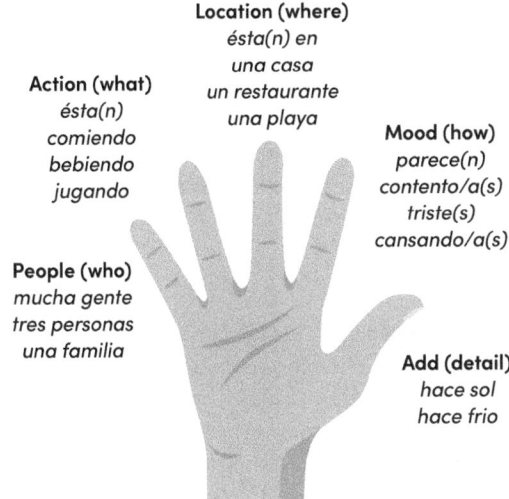

A Spanish example of the PALMA method

In some classrooms, it may be appropriate for students to simplify what they see using 'In the photo there is/are ...'. An example in Spanish may include:

- *En la foto hay una familia.*
- *En la foto hay cinco personas.*
- *En la foto hay un gato.*
- *En la foto hay una playa.*

Students now need to cover both photos. Train them to give at least one point per PALM(A) category across both photos.

Example:

En la primera foto hay una familia en la playa...

En la segunda foto veo a unos estudiantes en clase...

HACK #2

Use vocabulary and sentence starters with question prompts: To help students feel more confident, introduce common vocabulary and sentence starters related to typical photo-card topics (family, free time, school). For example, phrases like 'In the foreground, I can see ...' or 'It seems like they are ...' give students a strong foundation to begin their description. Create a 'photo-card toolkit' with phrases categorised by topic or theme, and have students practise using them in different contexts. Build in prompts that connect the two photos together and sentence starters like:

- *Ambas fotos muestran...*
- *Sin embargo, en la segunda foto...*

To help students generate ideas and focus their thoughts, we might provide a list of question prompts that guide their responses. These might include questions like 'What is happening in the photo?', 'What do you think the people are feeling?' or simply 'What do you see?'. By offering a structure, students are better able to organise their thoughts and provide coherent answers.

HACK #3

Create vocabulary banks and knowledge organisers: Students often struggle with the vocabulary needed to describe photos. We might support them by having them create vocabulary banks tailored to different types of photos or topics. For instance, if the photo depicts a scene at the beach, the vocabulary bank might include words like 'sea', 'sun', 'swimming', 'umbrella' or 'sunbathing'. This targeted vocabulary not only helps students describe the image but also equips them with useful words for real-life situations and the speaking exam.

HACK #4

Walk, talk and model: To help students understand how to approach the task, we can model the photo-card activity by thinking aloud as we describe a photo. This demonstrates the thought process behind organising ideas, choosing vocabulary and structuring responses. Using a visualiser or board may help with making note of specific vocabulary so that students may steal and share. By breaking down the task, we make it more accessible and give students a clear example to follow. Importantly, we might also make mistakes or change our minds about vocabulary use, which demonstrates to students that it is absolutely normal to develop thoughts in this way. As part of the modelling stage, we could also use the 'I do, we do, you do in pairs, and you do individually' model after every step to scaffold the activity. It is worth building in how to model the **transition into the unprepared conversation**, showing students how to expand beyond the photo.

HACK #5

Encourage peer support: Fluency is key in the photo-card task, and practising under timed conditions can help students manage their time more effectively. Pair, or trio, students and give them one minute to describe a photo to their partner. Make it a game. Make it fun. Make it low stakes. Afterward, switch roles. This exercise encourages students to think quickly, use the vocabulary they know and practise speaking without over-relying on notes, while having fun, making mistakes and learning from them and their peers. We might choose to display a timer on the board to keep students aware of how much time they have left, adding an element of real-time pressure to simulate exam conditions.

HACK #6

Incorporate technology for self-assessment: Technology can be a valuable tool for students to self-assess their speaking skills. Use apps or platforms that allow students to record themselves describing a photo. Joe Dale, an MFL consultant specialising in languages and technology, demonstrates this brilliantly. Once recorded, students can listen back, reflect on their use of vocabulary and pronunciation, and make changes. Free tools such as Vocaroo or qwicr are excellent for this purpose and should check if they gave at least one comment per photo and if they maintained fluency in the second part.

Conclusion

Photo-card tasks offer a dynamic way to integrate speaking skills into MFL lessons. By using structured approaches, pre-teaching vocabulary, encouraging peer interaction and incorporating scaffolding, we can ensure students feel supported and confident. These hacks not only enhance speaking fluency but also empower learners to engage with the target language in meaningful ways. It is a simple way to ensure success in one element of the speaking exam, that's for sure.

CHAPTER 9
CONVERSATION

The conversation task is one of the main elements of MFL teaching that allows students to be prepared for real interaction. It enables them to show how well they can express their ideas, give opinions and respond naturally to questions. In the new GCSEs, the conversation works slightly differently for Edexcel and AQA.

For Edexcel, the conversation comes after the photocard task and stays on the same thematic context. The teacher must begin the conversation using the thematic context given on the candidate's card, but the discussion can then naturally develop into other related themes if appropriate. This section is separate from the photo description and allows students to respond to questions using a range of vocabulary and grammar.

For AQA, the conversation is integrated into the photocard task and flows more like a natural discussion. After describing the photos, students continue speaking with the teacher about any topics within the prescribed theme, without a clear break into a new section. It focuses more on students speaking fluently and keeping the conversation going. This part of the task is called the unprepared conversation, and the teacher can ask about any of the three topic areas listed under the theme on the student's card. Students need to be ready to talk about a variety of ideas. The conversation task is designed to mirror authentic communicative situations, where speakers must express opinions, justify ideas and navigate spontaneous exchanges. While this may seem daunting for students, we can implement a number of strategies to ensure learners are well-prepared and confident. What matters is a proper balance between careful preparation and opportunities for spontaneity to prepare them for both planned and unplanned interaction.

 HACK #1

Introduce topics: The first step in preparing students for conversation tasks is ensuring they are comfortable with a range of topics. Begin by introducing common topics and themes early on, such as media, lifestyle, mental wellbeing, school life, family, environmental issues or technology. Use mind maps, brainstorming and encourage students to research these topics at home, in the target language, building up their vocabulary and awareness of key issues. By discussing these themes regularly in class through debates, group discussions or presentations, students will develop a deeper understanding of the subject matter, making it easier for them to engage during the formal conversation task.

HACK #2

Practice question-and-answer drills: Responding to unknown questions is often the most-intimidating part of the task. To build confidence, engage students regularly in Q&A drills. Start by having students work in pairs, where one starts with a short description and the other asks follow-up questions. Initially, these questions can be guided, for example, 'Why?' and 'Can you tell me more …?'.

As students become more comfortable, move towards unscripted questioning, preparing them to cope with unexpected topics. Encouraging peer-to-peer questioning develops active-listening skills that will be so crucial for the process of spontaneous exchanges.

HACK #3

Incorporate technology for self-assessment: One of the most effective ways to improve speaking is through self-assessment. Encourage students to record themselves asking and answering questions. After that, let them listen to themselves in order to reflect on their fluency, pronunciation and response to pressure. They can note areas for improvement, such as filling gaps with appropriate phrases or avoiding repetition. Recording also allows them to have a clearer focus for future practice based on peer feedback and teacher feedback where necessary.

HACK #4

Conversation chain: Have students form a circle or line and start a chain conversation based on a question or theme. Each student must respond to the previous speaker and then add something new. For example, if the topic is environmental issues, Student A says: "I think plastic pollution is a major issue." Student B replies: "I agree, especially in oceans. I also think deforestation is a problem." And so on. This promotes listening and extended speaking: key components of fluency.

HACK #5

Sentence starters aka Survival phrases: Give students a bank of useful sentence starters and conversation fillers. These could include phrases like:

"In my opinion..."

"What I mean is..."

"That's a difficult question, but..."

"Let me think..."

"I've never thought about that, but..."

Having access to these in early stages boosts spontaneity and helps students sound more natural while gaining time to think. Eventually, students internalise them and use them instinctively.

Conclusion

The speaking conversation activity in MFL teaching offers a great opportunity to develop students' prepared- and spontaneous-speaking skills. Familiarise the students with common topics and themes, practise Q&A drills, role play the simulation in unknown topic scenarios, and make students reflect. With these strategies, we will help our students gain the confidence to develop the skills necessary to be successful. Ultimately, these strategies help create a classroom environment where students are ready to engage with the target language in a dynamic and authentic way.

Reading
CHAPTER 10
READING ALOUD

> Madame Kowalska, an experienced French teacher, keeps facing one issue repeatedly: the unwillingness of her students to read aloud during their French lessons.
>
> You see, in Madame Kowalska's lively classroom, you will find a diverse group of students, each with their own distinct proficiency levels. Some students are confident when speaking French, while others still grapple with pronunciation and self-assurance. Despite Madame Kowalska's belief in the importance of reading aloud for improving language skills, she can't help but notice the hesitancy that creeps in when she mentions this activity.
>
> But Madame Kowalska is not one to back down from a challenge. She understands that reading aloud is not just about pronunciation; it is about building confidence, honing speaking skills and preparing her students for their speaking assessments. With a determination in her heart, Madame Kowalska sets out to tackle this issue and ignite a passion for speaking French in her classroom.

Madame Kowalska's class scenario reflects a common challenge faced by language teachers: overcoming students' reluctance to read aloud and speak out. As we navigate the issue, we need to recognise the importance of creating a supportive learning environment and implementing effective strategies to encourage student participation.

Reading aloud in MFL classrooms is crucial for several reasons:

- **It enhances pronunciation and intonation skills**: students can practise the sounds and rhythm of the new language in a controlled setting. This verbal practice helps them to develop a more natural accent and understand the phonetic nuances that are often overlooked in silent reading.
- **It boosts listening skills**: students can hear their peers and the teacher, gaining exposure to different voices and speech patterns. This auditory exposure

is essential for developing aural comprehension, an integral component of language proficiency.
- **It fosters greater engagement and confidence**: when students read aloud, they become more actively involved in the learning process, which can reduce anxiety and build self-efficacy in using the new language publicly. This active participation also creates a more interactive classroom environment, encouraging peer learning and collaboration.
- **It aids in improving fluency**: the repetitive nature of reading aloud helps to internalise vocabulary and grammatical structures. The act of articulating text forces students to process language at a pace similar to natural speech, which is beneficial for acquiring conversational skills.
- **It facilitates immediate feedback from teachers**: teachers can correct mispronunciations and offer guidance on improving reading skills.
- **It integrates multiple learning modalities**: including visual and auditory, enhancing overall language retention and comprehension. By combining these elements, reading aloud can become a powerful pedagogical tool that supports a holistic approach to language learning, ensuring students not only understand the written word but can also communicate it effectively.

Incorporating regular reading-aloud sessions in MFL classrooms is indispensable for developing well-rounded language competence. However, for reading aloud to be successful, it requires careful scaffolding and sensitive handling. One effective strategy is choral reading aloud, where students read along with the teacher while following the text, providing a model for pronunciation and intonation. It is important not to force very shy or weaker students to read until they feel ready, as this can increase anxiety and hinder their progress. Instead, gradually build their confidence by starting with just a short sentence or shorter sections to read. Paired reading can also be beneficial, as it reduces the stress of reading in front of the entire class by allowing students to practise in a more comfortable, supportive setting.

What are some of the effective strategies for practising reading aloud successfully?

HACK #1

Choral reading aloud: This specific example, shared by Barry Smith, provides an effective approach. To encourage your students to practise reading aloud effectively, he suggests following this sequence with a text at the appropriate level displayed on the board or, preferably, from a printed text with the lines numbered and reading with a ruler.

- The teacher reads the text aloud while students listen. Students follow the text with their rulers.
- The teacher reads the text in short sections. The teacher very explicitly draws attention to high-frequency patterns to ensure highly accurate pronunciation. The class repeats in unison following the teacher's very-explicit model. The teacher is highly vigilant. Small groups, individual rows, for example, are called upon to read aloud. This helps ensure everyone participates and pronounces accurately. Incorrect pronunciation is corrected, and patterns are highlighted so students recognise the repetitive nature of the TL. Once students learn these patterns, they no longer need to guess.
- The teacher displays a version of the text with some letters missing (i.e. double/triple vowel combinations or accented vowels) and the class practises choral reading again. Students will use their memory to fill in the gaps. The teacher should tailor the gaps to suit the class. Students often make mistakes with high-frequency vowel combinations and accented vowels. This technique anticipates and prevents these common errors.
- The teacher repeats the process with whole words replaced by initials only. So, 'je suis allé au cinéma' becomes 'j s a a c'. Scaffolding is being removed in stages, providing both support and challenge simultaneously.
- Whole-class reading, following the teacher's model, continues. Students also read aloud individually, or as an entire class simultaneously, at the teacher's signal. The task is timed, and the teacher circulates to listen to students' pronunciation. Students place their fingers in their ears as they read to become less self-conscious. This allows them to focus on their own speaking and block out the voices of their peers.

This structured approach transitions from highly-scaffolded activities to less-scaffolded ones. Over time, students become more adept at recognising the phonics of the TL. Retention and recall improve, becoming easier and more accurate. Confidence grows, and pronunciation of the new language becomes more precise on the first reading. Guesswork is replaced by a ready reference to familiar TL phonics. As students recycle language across various topics, they become increasingly independent and assured, demonstrating greater ease and accuracy.

HACK #2

Team reading-aloud challenge: This activity is excellent not only for reading but also for promoting attentive listening, teamwork and pronunciation skills, all while engaging students in a fun and collaborative environment. Setting it up:

- The teacher divides the class into two teams, assigning each student in each team a number (these are same, i.e. Team A1/Team B1, etc.). Students receive

a text to read, and each team starts with 20 points. The teacher flips a coin to determine which team begins reading.
- The teacher randomly selects a number, and the student with that number from the chosen team reads aloud. The opposing team listens for pronunciation errors. If they hear an error, a student from the opposing team raises their hand and, if all teammates agree, everyone raises their hands to indicate consensus.
- Scoring points:
  - Correct error spotting: if a genuine error is identified, the opposing team gains a point and can help the reader correct it.
  - Incorrect error spotting: if the word was pronounced correctly, the opposing team loses a point, and the reading team gains a point.
- Each time an error is correctly identified, the teams switch roles. The team that collects the most points at the end of the activity wins.

This activity might be more suitable for classes that are accustomed to reading aloud, are more confident and have a supportive and 'safe' learning environment.

HACK #3

Quiz, quiz, trade: This well-known Kagan strategy is one of those go-to activities that encourages students to read, speak and be active as they move around. Here is how to set it up and manage it effectively:

- The teacher prepares cards with sentences related to the chosen topic or story.
- The teacher hands out one card to each student.
- The teacher instructs students to pair up and stand facing each other, holding their cards.
- The teacher instructs students to take turns reading the sentences on their cards in the target language.
- The teacher listens actively while circulating among the pairs.
- After both students have read their sentences, they trade cards.
- Students then find a new partner. 'Available' students can raise their hands to locate each other. The teacher encourages students not to pair with the same person twice to help them expand their social circle.
- The teacher also participates in providing one-to-one interaction and monitors areas needing additional attention, such as pronunciation or intonation, which serves as formative assessment.
- Students repeat the process for a set amount of time.

HACK #4

Trap door: This activity is excellent as it engages not only reading skills but also listening and speaking skills. Setting it up:

- The teacher displays several sentences in the TL, each containing multiple possible options. These sentences can be shown on the board or on a sheet of paper.
- The teacher randomly selects one option for each sentence, and students then try to guess which ones were chosen.
- One student starts by reading the first sentence out loud. If they guess the option correctly, they proceed to the next sentence.
- If the student guesses incorrectly, the teacher invites another student to start from the beginning.
- This process continues until a student successfully reads through the entire paragraph by guessing all options correctly.
- This activity can also be completed in groups.

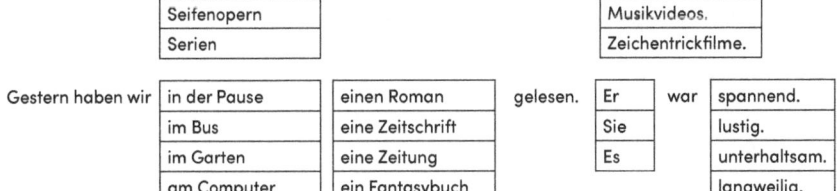

Trap door

This is a high-impact activity, as all students have to listen to each other carefully, to avoid repeating the same incorrect answer. The repetition involved also helps improve their pronunciation.

 HACK #5

Popcorn reading: In this classroom activity, students take turns reading aloud from a text displayed by the teacher. This activity can be conducted in pairs or with the whole class. To scaffold the activity, students can circle words they find tricky, and these can be discussed and practised chorally prior to reading aloud in front of the class. Each student reads just one or two words at a time initially, before 'popping' the reading to another student by calling out their name. The chosen student then continues reading from where the previous student left off. This approach keeps students engaged and attentive, as they must be ready to read at any moment. The goal is to make the passage flow smoothly with proper intonation, improving reading fluency, pronunciation and listening skills. As students become more comfortable, they can progress to reading full sentences in turns. You could also adapt this hack by controlling who reads, which prevents students from only choosing their friends or sticking to the same gender.

MORE HACKS

Here are some additional suggestions you might consider: partner reading, 'mime' reading (where the teacher demonstrates an action and a student responds with the corresponding sentence), silly voices, mood reading (where students incorporate different emotions while reading: sad, happy, angry, scared, etc.) and many more.

Conclusion

The practice of reading aloud not only enhances listening and speaking skills but also aids in vocabulary acquisition and retention. Through these activities, students are exposed to diverse linguistic structures, fostering an intuitive grasp of grammar and lexical patterns. Moreover, the interactive nature of reading aloud encourages active engagement, allowing students to refine pronunciation and intonation while honing their comprehension abilities. By integrating reading aloud into language-learning pedagogy, teachers can effectively nurture multifaceted language competencies, laying a robust foundation for linguistic proficiency and communication fluency.

CHAPTER 11
READING COMPREHENSION TASKS

Reading and comprehension are fundamental skills, playing a crucial role in students' ability to decipher and decode meaning, widen their vocabulary and engage with authentic texts. Developing these skills not only helps students understand the target language but also builds a bridge to cultural insights and real-world applications. However, reading in a foreign language can be challenging, as students must balance their knowledge and understanding of grammar, vocabulary and context clues to grasp meaning.

Effective teaching of reading and comprehension in MFL classrooms involves more than just providing texts for students to read. It requires a thoughtful approach that encourages active engagement, critical thinking, and the development of strategies to decipher unfamiliar words and phrases.

 HACK #1

Pre-teach vocabulary with context: One of the biggest barriers to reading comprehension in a foreign language is unfamiliar vocabulary. Rather than overwhelming students with long lists of new words, pre-teach key vocabulary in context. For example, if the text is about travelling, introduce essential words like 'ticket', 'station' or 'departure', but also show how they function within a sentence. We might use visuals or short phrases to embed these words into a meaningful context. This helps students feel more confident when they encounter the vocabulary in the text and allows them to focus on comprehension rather than decoding individual words.

 HACK #2

Teach skimming and scanning: Skimming and scanning are invaluable techniques for improving reading fluency. Skimming involves quickly reading through a text to grasp the main idea, while scanning focuses on finding specific information, for example, dates, names or facts. Teach students these techniques through timed activities. For example, give them a short article and ask them to find the gist within a minute (skimming), or have them locate specific details such as facts or key points (scanning). These exercises train students to manage their reading efficiently and reduce the pressure of understanding every single word.

HACK #3

Break down texts into manageable chunks: Long texts can overwhelm students, especially those still building their reading stamina in a foreign language. Break up the text into smaller sections and focus on understanding each part before moving on to the next. After reading a chunk, engage students in summarising the gist of the section in their own words or discussing key points with a partner. This step-by-step approach prevents students from becoming discouraged by the length of the material and allows for focused comprehension checks along the way.

HACK #4

Encourage common sense and resilience: Rather than having students immediately resort to a dictionary when encountering unfamiliar words, encourage them to guess the meaning from context, using their knowledge of cognates their ability to break down compound nouns (in German) and common sense! Teach them how to look for clues in the sentence itself or surrounding sentences that might give insight into the word's meaning. For example, if a student doesn't know the word 'car' but sees it in a sentence like 'They drove their car to work every day', they can infer its meaning based on the action. This skill is essential for building reading independence, as it allows students to engage with more complex texts without being reliant on external aids.

HACK #5

Use authentic texts with scaffolding: Introducing authentic texts, such as news articles, stories or blogs written by native speakers, exposes students to real-world language use and cultural context. However, without proper support, these texts may feel daunting. Provide scaffolding by offering pre-reading glossaries with essential vocabulary and phrases from the text. Use guiding questions (in English or TL) to direct students to focus on the key points in the text. You could also offer comprehension prompts, such as sentence starters or multiple-choice questions, to check for understanding (see the example on the next page).

> An example text: *'El presidente viajó a la ciudad para participar en una conferencia sobre el cambio climático. Durante el evento, destacó la importancia de reducir las emisiones de carbono para proteger el medio ambiente.'*
>
> Activity: Choose the correct option in each case.
>
> The president travelled to _____.
>
> a) attend a climate change conference
> b) visit family
> c) discuss a trade agreement.
>
> The goal of the conference was to highlight the importance of _____.
>
> a) reducing carbon emissions
> b) raising taxes
> c) promoting new technology.

You could ask students to find words in the text that are similar to words in their native language – cognates (e.g. *'conferencia'*/conference, *'importancia'*/importance). This helps build their confidence and shows them how to leverage cognates for comprehension. By progressively introducing different types of support, students can engage deeply with the authentic text while still having the necessary tools to understand it fully. As they gain confidence, the support can be gradually reduced, helping them become more independent readers.

Conclusion

Reading and comprehension in a foreign language can be challenging but incredibly rewarding when approached with the right strategies. By pre-teaching vocabulary in context, teaching skimming and scanning techniques, using comprehension questions to promote critical thinking, breaking texts into manageable chunks, and encouraging students to guess meaning from context, we can help students develop the skills needed to confidently engage with texts in the target language. These techniques foster both understanding and independence, ensuring that students are not just reading but truly comprehending and applying what they learn in meaningful ways.

CHAPTER 12
TRANSLATION TO ENGLISH

Teaching translation from a target language to English can be a highly effective method for deepening language comprehension and honing communication skills. Translation exercises challenge students to consider language on a nuanced level, building an understanding of both vocabulary and cultural context. By bridging languages, students also engage with both cultures, learning that translation is not merely about words, but about meaning. Below are five practical hacks to encourage translation skills and make it a dynamic, rewarding part of MFL instruction.

HACK #1

Micro-translations: Begin with 'micro-translations' – short phrases or idiomatic expressions that provide a manageable but meaningful translation exercise. Encourage students to use their common sense; their understanding of the context. Are there any cognates? What are their predictions about the text? Ask students to translate a single sentence, proverb or line of dialogue from a foreign language text into English, focusing on retaining the phrase's tone and implied meaning rather than translating word-for-word. This approach introduces students to translation at a digestible level and emphasises the importance of context. Encourage students to discuss their translation choices and explain how they preserved the meaning of the original.

HACK #2

Comparative media to explore nuances: In a world where our students are experts in the realms of technology and seemingly always 'switched on', one of the most engaging ways to teach translation is through the comparison of media, such as news headlines from social media, movie dialogues or song lyrics, in both languages. This approach brings translation into real-life scenarios and shows students how meaning can shift between languages based on cultural and contextual factors. Ask students to translate a short news headline or song lyric and then compare it with an English translation. This exercise fosters discussion on why certain words or phrases were chosen and how this impacts the overall message.

HACK #3

Pair translation with cultural context: Translation without cultural understanding can lead to literal but incorrect interpretations. Make translation exercises culturally rich by pairing the texts with a brief cultural overview. For example, when translating French poetry or Spanish proverbs, discuss the historical or cultural context first. This helps students grasp underlying meanings or references that are tied to the culture of the target language. Such awareness will help them recognise when literal translations fall short and encourage them to make choices that respect the cultural nuances of the original text.

 HACK #4

Encourage peer review and collaborative translation: Translation can be challenging, so building a collaborative environment in the classroom is essential. Assign a translation task and then have students work in pairs or small groups to compare their results. Students can exchange feedback, discuss challenges and consider each other's translation choices. This peer review not only encourages students to see translation as a creative, collaborative activity but also helps them learn from one another's insights, improving their own approach to language.

 HACK #5

Integrate technology for real-world practice: Unpopular opinion incoming! It can be helpful to incorporate translation apps and tools into the classroom to give students insight into real-world translation practices. For example, students can use a translation app to see an initial version of a translated text. Show them how inaccurate it can be! Then edit it to make it more accurate and culturally appropriate. Encourage them to identify errors or areas where the app failed to capture context, as this will help them to think critically about the role of human understanding in translation. By practising with technology, students also gain digital-literacy skills that are invaluable in today's globalised world and also, just maybe, prevent them from using translation apps for their homework!

A nod to translation activities

There are so many brilliant and effective activities in the MFL community, including 'ping pong' translation inspired by Dr Gianfranco Conti, or 'running translation' or 'mosaic translation' inspired by Kim Davies. Activities like these are essential for building not only students' skills but also their self-belief. If students encounter key vocabulary and structures often enough, they start to feel a sense of confidence and develop a more natural ability in using them across all their language skills.

Conclusion

No matter the choice of activity, effective translation teaching requires that students move beyond simple word substitution and engage deeply with the meanings and contexts behind words. By emphasising micro-translations, comparative media, cultural understanding, collaborative exercises and technology, teachers can make translation a meaningful and engaging part of language learning. These hacks not only help students become more proficient translators but also more culturally aware individuals who appreciate the complexities and beauty of language.

Writing
CHAPTER 13
DICTATION

Mrs Rodriguez is a Spanish teacher embarking on her first year in the profession. Full of energy, ideas and enthusiasm, she is determined to improve her students' listening and writing abilities through engaging dictation exercises. With a natural flair for creativity, Mrs Rodriguez is on a mission to make dictation sessions both captivating and impactful while teaching her very first Year 9 Spanish class.

In her classroom, each student brings their own unique strengths and areas for improvement. While some students demonstrate a keen ear for pronunciation, others may find spelling or retaining auditory information challenging. Despite these differences, Mrs Rodriguez fully appreciates the vital role dictation plays in developing her students' listening comprehension and writing skills.

Yet, as a novice teacher, Mrs Rodriguez finds herself struggling with ideas on how to effectively teach dictation and provide engaging activities, especially for her predominantly male class, many of whom harbour a dislike for any kind of spelling practice.

As a new teacher, Mrs Rodriguez likely encounters challenges stemming from her limited experience in effectively engaging a diverse group of students. Balancing varying skill levels in dictation exercises, ensuring they are neither too easy nor too difficult, presents a particular challenge as she strives to find the 'sweet spot'. Additionally, she must devise creative ways to make spelling and listening tasks engaging for those less inclined to participate. The pressure to deliver enjoyable learning experiences while meeting learning objectives can be daunting for a novice teacher, potentially affecting her confidence. Nevertheless, this chapter concentrates on how we can overcome these obstacles.

What is dictation?

Dictation is a teaching method where the teacher reads aloud a set of sentences or a paragraph in the TL and students listen to this spoken language and transcribe it accurately. It is an often-underestimated tool, which holds significant benefits in the modern language classroom.

What benefits does dictation offer?

- **Dictation enhances listening skills**: when students listen attentively to spoken language, they improve their ability to distinguish sounds, intonations and nuances, which are crucial for mastering a new language. This practice helps in developing an 'ear' for the language, fostering better comprehension and pronunciation.
- **Dictation supports spelling and grammar learning**: as students transcribe what they hear, they reinforce their understanding of spelling conventions and grammatical structures. This active engagement with the language helps solidify correct forms and usage, aiding in both written and spoken communication.
- **Dictation aids in vocabulary retention**: hearing words in context and writing them down helps embed these words more deeply in the learner's long-term memory. It also provides a context for vocabulary usage, making it easier for students to recall and apply new words appropriately in different situations.
- **Dictation serves as a tool for refining inference skills**: this is achieved through activities like dictating passages with blank spaces for students to complete using contextual cues. This approach not only strengthens listening and comprehension skills but also nurtures critical thinking and contextual comprehension.
- **Dictation exercises can be tailored to different proficiency levels**: this makes it a versatile tool for differentiated instruction. For beginners, simple sentences can introduce basic vocabulary and structures, while advanced learners can tackle more complex passages that challenge their listening and writing skills.
- **Dictation fosters concentration and mental agility**: the need to listen carefully, process information and transcribe accurately requires focused attention, thereby enhancing cognitive functions such as memory and attention to detail.
- **Lastly, dictation promotes active learning and participation**: it engages students in a dynamic process, transforming passive listening into an interactive task. This engagement not only makes the learning process more enjoyable but also increases retention and understanding, making dictation a valuable asset in the modern language classroom.

What role does dictation play in an MFL classroom, and what significance does it hold?

In recent times, dictation has gained increased popularity in England, particularly with its inclusion in the new GCSE curriculum. The first examination featuring dictation is scheduled for 2026. The French, German and Spanish GCSE subject content (DfE, 2022) specifies that students must:

> undertake dictation of short, spoken extracts (including some vocabulary from outside the vocabulary list) with credit for accurate spelling.

The dictation task is essential for assessing SSCs. Both of the exam boards AQA and Edexcel (Pearson Education) limit the vocabulary to only what is necessary for the task and this includes two unfamiliar words that students are still likely to recognise based on their SSC knowledge. They also allow full marks for these words, even if the spelling is not completely accurate.

What are some effective strategies for integrating dictation into language lessons?

Here are some proven classroom strategies – hacks that effectively enhance learning outcomes while fostering enjoyment.

HACK #1

Classic sentence dictation: Setting it up:

- The teacher introduces the sentences to the students using choral repetition.
- The teacher dictates sentences or a short paragraph to the students.
- The teacher starts slowly, with clear pauses between words, then gradually increases the speed and starts joining words using liaison.
- Students write down on their mini whiteboards what they hear in the TL.
- After counting to three, students show the teacher their written work.
- The teacher checks for understanding immediately and adapts their dictations based on the students' responses.

HACK #2

Substitution dictation: Here is a fun twist on a standard dictation activity that also provides an extra challenge. Setting it up:

- The teacher selects some keywords from the text.

- The teacher replaces these keywords with some humorous alternatives in TL such as 'apple', 'cake', etc.
- The teacher dictates the sentences/text using these substituted words.
- Students listen and write sentences.
- After the dictation, the teacher encourages students to guess what the original words should be based on the context.

HACK #3

Running/walking dictation: Setting it up:

- The teacher distributes texts around the classroom.
- Students pair up, with one taking the role of the 'scribe', stationed at their desk with paper and pen, while the other acts as the 'runner', moving to the text, memorising a section, then returning to dictate it to the scribe. (Alternatively, this activity can be conducted as a running/walking dictation, with groups of 3–4 students in each group.)
- This activity promotes physical activity, memory retention and comprehension assessment. It serves as a comprehensive exercise for listening, writing, speaking and reading skills improvement.

HACK #4

Gapped dictation: To provide additional scaffolding, I would progress to this activity after the class has done some delayed dictation, where students see the sentence first. Next, students hear the same sentence with one word variation. They should identify this word, and then write it correctly. Finally, students move on to gapped dictation. This level of scaffolding can be particularly useful for languages like French, where identifying correct phonemes may be more challenging compared to German or Spanish. Setting it up:

- The teacher provides sentences/a text with certain words missing.
- The teacher reads the sentences/text aloud, and students fill in the spaces with the words they hear.
- This dictation activity enhances vocabulary and grammatical-structure recognition, sharpens focus on specific language components and tests students' knowledge in a practical context.

Writing Chapter 13 DICTATION

> Example:
>
> Original sentence: *Los sábados por la tarde, suelo quedar con mis amigos porque me ayuda a desconectar y relajarme.*
>
> Student A:
>
> *Los _____ por la tarde, _____ quedar con _____ amigos porque _____ ayuda _____ desconectar y _____.*
>
> Student B:
>
> *Los sábados por la _____, suelo quedar _____ mis amigos _____ me _____ a desconectar _____ relajarme.*

 HACK # 5

Dictogloss (Wajnryb, 1990): This activity involves learners reconstructing a short text by listening and noting down key words, which serve as a foundation for reconstruction. It is particularly beneficial because it engages multiple skills and systems. Learners not only practise listening, writing and speaking (especially in group settings) but also utilise vocabulary, grammar and discourse systems to accomplish the task. Setting it up:

- The teacher will read aloud a passage. Students pay close attention but do not take any notes.
- Students write down as many words as they can recall from the passage.
- Students put their pens down and listen to the passage again.
- Students pair up with a classmate and combine both of their recollections to reconstruct the passage.
- Students put their pens down again and listen to the passage once more.
- Students attempt another reconstruction using their combined notes.
- The teacher distributes a jumbled-up version of the passage.
- Students use this and their notes to verify/finalise their reconstruction of the passage.
- Students write a reflection: What aspects did they find challenging? Why?

 HACK #6

Paired/partner dictation: Similar to the gapped dictation, this activity is completed in pairs (student A and student B) and led by students not by the teacher. Setting it up:

- The teacher provides the students with two examples of the same text, each text having different words missing

- Student A reads their text aloud so that student B can fill in the missing words in their version.
- Student B then reads their text aloud so that student A can fill in the missing words in their version.
- Students check their answers.
- The teacher circulates and listens to students' pronunciation and checks the accuracy of their spelling.

Paired dictation

Student A	Student B
_____, je m'appelle Julien. J'ai _____ ans. J'habite à Rennes, c'est une _____ en Bretagne, dans l'ouest ____ ____ France. C'est _____ grande. L'année dernière, ma famille et moi, nous avons voyagé en _____ et aussi en bateau. En _____, nous avons fait du snowboard.	Bonjour, je _____ Julien. J'ai douze _____. J'habite à Rennes, c'est une ville en Bretagne, _____ l'ouest de la France. C'est très grande. L'année dernière, ma famille et moi, nous avons voyagé en voiture et aussi en _____. En plus, _____ avons fait du snowboard.

Challenge: Translate the paragraph into English in your book.

 MORE HACKS

Additional activities you could try are picture dictation, grammar-focused dictation, translation dictation, mad dictation, minimal-pairs dictation, alternate sentences dictation and many more.

Conclusion

Incorporating dictation exercises into the MFL classroom proves highly effective. As evidenced by the activities above, through dictation, students engage actively with language structure, spelling and listening comprehension. This strategy fosters linguistic accuracy, enhances vocabulary retention and reinforces grammar rules in a dynamic learning environment.

CHAPTER 14
PHOTO TASK

Sophie looks down at the photo task sheet on her desk and lets out a quiet sigh. It's that part of the lesson again, GCSE-style writing practice. She's never found it easy. Even though it's only four short sentences now, Sophie always feels unsure where to start, what to say or how to make sure her grammar is right. However, this time, she came prepared. Her teacher, Mr Chen, had gone through a new way of planning responses that made things feel a bit more manageable. Together, the class looked at example answers and spotted what made them successful: simple but accurate language, clear short sentences and good use of vocabulary they already knew.

When Mr Chen hands out the photo task, Sophie's heart still races a little, but she reminds herself of the steps: look at the picture; think of four simple things I can say about it; keep it clear; keep it correct.

She picks up her pen and gets started. One sentence at a time. No overthinking. Just sticking to what she practised. By the time the timer goes off, Sophie feels a small wave of relief. It's done and, for once, she's not second-guessing herself. She's pretty sure she managed four complete sentences, checked her verbs and spelling, and kept things simple. It might not be perfect, but it feels like progress.

Sophie's situation is a familiar one. Lots of students find the photo task harder than it seems. Even though it only asks for four or five short sentences (depending on the exam board), it still requires confidence, control and quick thinking, especially under exam pressure.

In Sophie's case, she hadn't missed out part of the answer this time – giving an opinion is no longer a requirement of this task. Instead, her main hurdle was knowing how to get started and what kind of language to use. Like many students, she worried about accuracy and froze when trying to form full sentences on the spot.

This can come down to several things: uncertainty around sentence structure, grammar, gaps in vocabulary, nerves or just not knowing what makes a 'good enough' answer. For students like Sophie, building confidence through simple strategies and lots of practice can make a huge difference.

What stood out in Sophie's lesson was the shift in approach. Rather than diving straight into writing, the class looked at how to break the task into manageable chunks, how to spot patterns in model answers and how to reuse familiar sentence frames in a flexible way.

Not every student will come with the same level of motivation or determination as Sophie. Some will need more structure. Some will need more encouragement. But all students can benefit from being shown how to plan and write short, effective answers in a way that feels achievable. This chapter will examine examples of effective strategies to support our students in achieving success in this aspect of their written exam.

GCSE photo tasks: what they look like now

Here is a quick summary of what the photo-based writing tasks now involve.

Edexcel specification (Pearson Education, 2024):

- Task: Write four short sentences to describe a photo.
- No opinion needed.
- Worth 8 marks.
- Foundation tier only.

AQA specification (AQA, 2024):

- Task: Write five short sentences based on a photo.
- No opinion needed.
- Worth 10 marks.
- Foundation tier only.

Now that all students are working towards the new 2024 GCSE, it is a great time to help them build solid foundations for success in tasks like this one. The photo description is a perfect opportunity to develop sentence-building confidence, practise some core vocabulary and apply grammar in a low-pressure way. In the next section, we will share examples of simple scaffolds we have used in our classrooms to support learners like Sophie, helping them plan quickly, write clearly and feel more in control of their own writing.

HACK #1

Sentence-building grid: This is a structured grid populated with useful vocabulary for the picture-based task following the PAL(MW) (People/Action/Location/Mood/Weather or Why) acronym (similar to that mentioned in Chapter 8). It is designed to support students with scaffolded responses. It offers initial support, which is especially helpful for learners who may find it challenging to structure and construct their responses. It presents varying levels of support. This support is gradually removed to promote independence.

Setting it up:

- The teacher shows and distributes the sentence grid to students.
- The teacher directs students to highlight all the vocabulary they know.
- Students practise the grid chorally with the teacher in class.
- Students strengthen their learning at home through assigned homework.
- In the next lesson, the teacher supplies students with a sentence grid displaying only the first column.
- As part of their retrieval practice, students are tasked by the teacher to fill in the grid with as much vocabulary as they can recall for each section.

HACK #2

Mosaic grid: This task provides scaffolded support by giving students a picture, a description of the picture in their first language and a grid with a mosaic translation in the second language. Using the grid, students reconstruct the text. To increase difficulty, 'distractors' can be included. The next task could be a gap-fill exercise where students are given the text with some words missing. To further decrease scaffolding, students could be given only the first letters of each word to reconstruct the target language text. This progressively increases the challenge of the task. This strategy can also be used to help prepare for the speaking component of the GCSE.

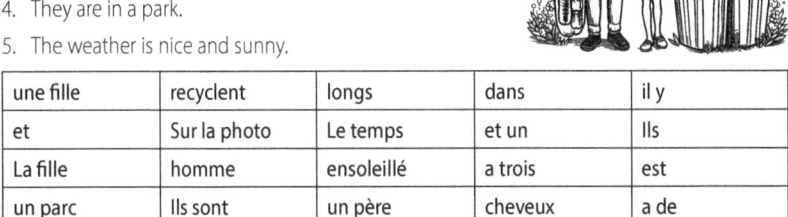

Décris la photo et donne ton avis sur l'environnement.

1. On the photo there are three people: a father, a daughter and an old man.
2. The girl has long blond hair.
3. They are recycling rubbish.
4. They are in a park.
5. The weather is nice and sunny.

une fille	recyclent	longs	dans	il y
et	Sur la photo	Le temps	et un	Ils
La fille	homme	ensoleillé	a trois	est
un parc	Ils sont	un père	cheveux	a de
personnes	blonds	beau	des déchets	vieil

An example of a mosaic grid for the photo task

HACK #3

PALMW: This activity, similar to the sentence-building grid, offers a scaffolding for the weakest students. It is coherently structured to reduce cognitive load by providing a simple visual and minimising distractions. It is organised in two stages: first, providing full support, and second, offering just an acronym or a picture prompt. This strategy could be used to speaking preparation too.

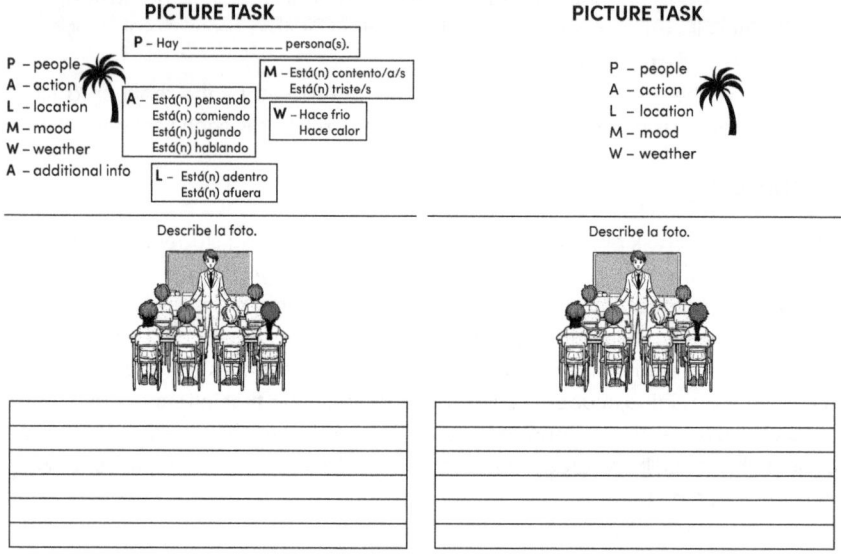

Activity: Hannah Pinkham (adapted)

Conclusion

Photo tasks in the GCSE writing paper are a great way to help students get creative with their language. Just like in Chapter 8, where we explored simple strategies to support speaking, this task gives learners the chance to apply what they know in a meaningful and engaging way. By using clear structures, teaching key vocabulary up front, working on short writing tasks together and providing scaffolding, we can help students feel more confident and capable. These approaches not only boost accuracy and fluency, but they also help learners connect more personally with the language. When we build photo tasks into our lessons regularly, we're giving students the tools they need to do well in the real exam.

CHAPTER 15
EXTENDED WRITING TASK

As Ms Okonkwo sits at her desk, marking yet another set of extended writing tasks from her class, a wave of frustration washes over her. Week after week, she had tirelessly drilled her students on grammatical concepts such as tenses, adjectival endings, gender agreement, subjunction and word order, only to find that her students have yet again struggled to apply them in their writing. The task at hand, requiring students to write 80–90 words, seemed simple enough on the surface. Yet time and time again her students struggle to transfer their knowledge from the classroom to the page. As she reads through the latest batch of essays, Ms Okonkwo cannot help but feel disheartened. The sentences are riddled with errors, the tenses are muddled, adjectives are misplaced and gender agreements are non-existent. It is as if her hours of teaching had fallen on deaf ears. With a heavy sigh, Ms Okonkwo knows she needs to explore new teaching strategies and provide additional scaffolding to help her students bridge the gap between theory and practice.

Inspired by a colleague's mention of using 'live' modelling to support students with this task, she is confident that with careful planning, breaking the task into small steps, she can guide her students to master the skill of extended writing and unleash their full potential.

In the landscape of MFL education, teachers like Ms Okonkwo often face one significant challenge: the gap between students' theoretical knowledge and its practical application. Ms Okonkwo faces this issue head-on as she observes her students struggling to apply grammatical concepts to their extended writing tasks. Despite her thorough and carefully planned lessons on tenses, adjectival endings, gender agreement, subjunction and word order, as well as extensive classroom practice, she is disheartened to find that her students' written work often lacks coherence and is riddled with many mistakes.

Ms Okonkwo's situation mirrors a common dilemma encountered by many language teachers worldwide. The seemingly simple task of composing 80–90 or 130–150 words of cohesive writing becomes a hurdle for students, testing their ability to internalise and utilise language skills beyond the classroom. Despite the teachers' efforts, the disconnect between declarative (factual, instructional) and procedural (applied) knowledge persists, leaving both teachers and students frustrated.

This challenge goes beyond MFL instruction, affecting a wide array of subjects and fields. Whether in mathematics, science, literature or other disciplines, students often face difficulties in transferring and applying their knowledge to different scenarios and contexts.

Why is it important to teach writing skills?

Teaching writing skills from the start is crucial because it lays a solid foundation for effective communication and students' academic success. Investing time in developing these skills at KS3 ensures that students build a strong grasp of grammar, structure and expression early on, making the transition to KS4 and beyond smoother and more effective. When students enter KS4 with well-honed writing abilities, they are better equipped to tackle complex extended writing tasks and exams, reducing the need for remedial efforts and allowing for a deeper focus on subject or course content.

This early investment not only enhances students' self-efficacy and competence in writing but also alleviates the pressure on teachers to 'play catch up' on essential skills that should have been mastered earlier. As a result, a proactive approach at KS3 can lead to more cohesive and comprehensive learning experiences throughout a student's language journey.

Where do we begin? How should we approach it?

We can begin at KS3 by implementing a variety of engaging and structured techniques tailored to developing writing skills in younger students. This could include incorporating strategies and activities such as dictation (i.e. delayed or running dictation, as mentioned in Chapter 13) to improve listening and transcription skills, reinforcing the connection between spoken and written language. Encouraging students to write short sentences and paragraphs helps them grasp basic syntax and punctuation, while scaffolded translation activities can enhance their vocabulary and understanding of sentence structure.

Additionally, guiding students through extended writing tasks that are formatted similarly to the style of a GCSE exam can also be an effective strategy. This approach includes the teacher guiding them by providing structured support through 'live' modelling, followed by students tackling these tasks independently, mirroring the layout and expectations of the actual exam. When students familiarise themselves with the format early on, they become more confident and adept at approaching longer writing. By establishing these foundational practices at KS3, we can ensure students are well-prepared for the more advanced writing tasks they will encounter in KS4.

At KS4, embracing structured writing approaches can also prove advantageous in breaking down the writing process for our students. This can be particularly helpful for students who may struggle due to limitations in their working memory, especially when it comes to transferring and applying their knowledge. By providing clear and organised frameworks, such as structured/scaffolded writing tasks, we can support students, particularly those with cognitive challenges, in understanding and executing writing assignments more effectively. Here are several impactful ideas that have proven to be effective in our classrooms:

HACK #1

Deconstruction model: This activity involves the teacher providing students with a text in the TL and prompting them to identify examples of adjectives, frequency or time phrases, opinions, connectives, past tense, present tense, future tense, conditional and other linguistic elements. By engaging in this exercise, students are encouraged to consider their writing in terms of the criterion of using a variety of language, as outlined in the mark scheme. They can highlight the different language elements in the text using different colours. It is essentially a text analysis.

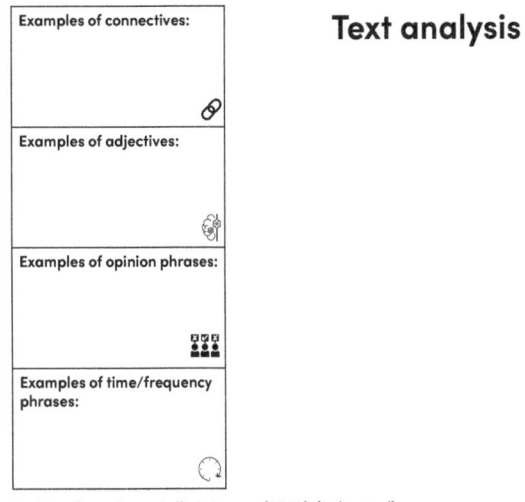

Activity from Dannielle Warren (2019) (adapted)

HACK #2

Comparison models: In this activity, the teacher presents students with two models/worked examples; one is higher quality than the other. Students are tasked with evaluating which example is better and explaining their reasoning. The teacher may supply students with the mark scheme, but it is important they understand and can apply it correctly. Students can work individually or in pairs. Afterwards, they share their insights as part of a class discussion.

> **Example: Text A (grade 5)**
>
> Je travaille dans une bibliothèque parce que c'est amusant. J'aime beaucoup les livres parce que je suis passionné de lecture. La meilleure partie, c'est que je peux lire avec les enfants, même s'ils sont parfois trop bruyants. De plus, mon travail est super parce que mes collègues sont à la fois drôles et gentils.
>
> La semaine dernière, je suis allé faire du shopping avec ma copine pour acheter une jupe à rayures. Si j'en avais l'opportunité, je travaillerais comme scientifique, car j'adore la biologie.
>
> Écris-moi bientôt,
>
> Étienne
>
> **Example: Text B (grade 7–9)**
>
> Bonjour Pierre,
>
> Je travaille dans une bibliothèque parce que c'est amusant. Je pense que les livres sont toujours fascinants parce que je suis un rat de bibliothèque. La meilleure partie, c'est que je peux lire avec les enfants, même s'ils peuvent parfois être trop bruyants. De plus, mon travail est génial parce que mes collègues sont à la fois amusants et sympathiques. La semaine dernière, je suis allé faire du shopping avec ma copine pour acheter une jupe rayée. Si j'en avais l'occasion, je travaillerais comme scientifique, car je trouve la biologie fascinante.
>
> Écris-moi bientôt,
>
> Étienne

 HACK #3

Models of excellence: When used alongside comparison and deconstruction models, models of excellence (also referred to as WAGOLLs, or What a Good One Looks Like) can serve as scaffolds for students in the initial stages, demonstrating the standards they should aspire to achieve.

Writing Chapter 15 EXTENDED WRITING TASK

Querido Pablo,

Espero que estés bien. En este momento, estoy trabajando como camarera en un restaurante grande y moderno, y creo que este trabajo es bastante bueno porque recibo un buen salario. Sin embargo, también hay muchos inconvenientes, y a veces los clientes son muy malos y mezquinos, por lo que mi trabajo puede ser realmente agotador. Aun así, quiero trabajar aquí más tiempo porque quiero a mis compañeros. Todos son muy agradables.

La semana pasada fui de compras con mis amigos, y fue muy divertido porque el clima estaba agradable y cálido. Comimos un delicioso helado y también caminamos por el parque. ¡Qué bien! Después de eso, decidimos comprar ropa. ¡Tenía que comprar unos jeans!

En el futuro, me gustaría convertirme en veterinaria porque amo a los animales, y así puedo pasar todo el día con muchos animales diferentes. Creo que sería realmente genial.

Un abrazo,

Alejandra

HACK #4

Live modelling: The teacher guides students through the learning process, demonstrating how to execute the task effectively and emphasising the underlying thought processes. This is accomplished through physically engaging in the activity while using a visualiser. The teacher models the approach to the task by highlighting connections to previous learning, vocabulary and structures, as well as annotating the task to aid understanding. Encouraging self-efficacy, the teacher demonstrates proofreading and modelling metacognitive regulation, including planning before the task, monitoring during and evaluating afterwards. Additionally, students are shown how to construct their own work and are not allowed to copy or make notes during modelling. Remaining actively engaged, students provide suggestions, correct deliberate mistakes made by the teacher and offer vocabulary/structure improvements. The teacher verbalises explanations not only of 'what' to do but also 'why' and 'how', including guidance on when to begin a new paragraph, how to create a plan and how to assess their work.

HACK # 5

Co-construction model: Following the 'I do/we do/you do' model, after the 'I do' phase, where the teacher 'live' models the task, the next step is co-construction, or 'we do'. In this phase, an example is created together as a class using a visualiser. It is important that students avoid just simply copying what the teacher writes, instead, there should be continuous questioning and interaction, with adjustments made along the way. For example, if a mistake is made, it is acknowledged and corrected through dialogue, such as, 'I'm not sure about this word – what would be better? Can you suggest another – better – word?'. This also presents an opportunity to use the cold-call technique.

After this thorough, guided and deliberate practice, our students should be prepared for the independent 'you do' phase. During this phase, students apply the discussed models as examples to complete their tasks autonomously.

Conclusion

Developing strong writing skills is important for our students' success. Throughout this chapter, we have looked at a variety of effective strategies to cultivate these skills. From structured approaches to guided practice, we have emphasised the importance of providing scaffolding and support to students at every stage of their learning journey. By incorporating techniques such as guided practice, live modelling, co-construction and independent practice, we have aimed to instil confidence and competence in our students. Moving forward, it is essential to continue refining these strategies, adapting them to meet the diverse needs of our students.

CHAPTER 16
TRANSLATION TO TARGET LANGUAGE

> As Zain sits at his desk staring at the English sentences before him, he feels a growing frustration. Despite hours spent memorising vocabulary and studying grammar rules, he struggles to translate the sentences smoothly and accurately. Each sentence appears to mock him, refusing to form a coherent structure. The complexities of German verb endings, noun genders, cases and sentence structures evade him, resulting in translation attempts that are clumsy, disjointed, often word by word, and riddled with gaps. Zain's mind races as he wracks his brain for the right words and phrases, but they don't seem to be there. The more he tries to remember them, the more they slip through his 'fingers'.
>
> With each passing minute, Zain's irritation intensifies. He is aware that the words and rules are somewhere in his head, but he just can't recall them ...

As already addressed in Chapter 12, translation can be a delicate process that involves striking a balance between preserving the essence of the original language and breathing new life into it in the TL. It entails deciphering the meaning in one language and then conveying it accurately in another. This task can prove quite challenging, particularly when dealing with subtle cultural nuances or idiomatic expressions. It is important to note that no two translations will ever be entirely identical, especially when tackling longer passages. The manner in which translations are rendered often hinges on the skill, interpretation and creativity of the translator.

The frustrations faced by students like Zain highlight the intricate challenges inherent in this process. Students often find translation from their native language to the TL more challenging and difficult due to various barriers they encounter.

One significant barrier is the difference in linguistic structures between languages, including grammar rules, syntax and sentence construction. Translating often requires a deep understanding of both languages and the ability to navigate these differences effectively.

Additionally, as mentioned earlier, cultural nuances and idiomatic expressions pose challenges because they often lack direct equivalents in the TL. This requires students to not only grasp the literal meaning of words but also understand the cultural context behind them.

Moreover, ambiguity in language and the presence of multiple possible translations for a single word or phrase can complicate the process. Another obstacle is the lack of vocabulary, as students may struggle to know or find the right words to express the intended meaning accurately.

Finally, individual proficiency levels and familiarity with the TL also play a crucial role, with students at lower proficiency levels facing greater difficulty in conveying meaning accurately. Translation skills are important for students as they facilitate effective communication across languages and cultures, allowing us to bridge linguistic barriers and interact with people from diverse backgrounds.

To support students with translation, teachers can implement various strategies tailored to address the challenges they face.

What strategies can we employ to assist our students with translation into the TL?

When tackling the translation of simple sentences or short paragraphs, a skill introduced to students in KS3, there exist numerous ways to support their confidence and self-efficacy in this task. Following a comprehensive language processing phase, the use of scaffolds, such as employing various translation strategies, can effectively diversify students' learning experiences and maintain their focus and motivation. These strategies offer various levels of support, accommodating the diverse needs of students and ensuring every one of them can thrive. They are pivotal for nurturing a culture of confidence and competence: the 'I can do' attitude within the classroom. Introducing an element of competition to translation tasks can often heighten students' motivation, particularly among boys. However, the element of a competition can also be a cause of stress and anxiety, so knowing our students is particularly important.

Many of the translation activities discussed below are also applicable to GCSE students, particularly given that most GCSE classes consist of mixed-attainment levels. Students may require varying levels of support to enhance their confidence in translation skills.

Scaffolded tasks play a pivotal role in cultivating students' confidence and self-belief. As many language structures are repetitive, such as 'there is/are', 'I would like' or 'I find', repeated exposure enables students to incorporate these naturally into other language skills as well.

The following are examples of strategies we can deploy to support students in developing their translation skills.

HACK #1

Pre-translation preparation: When faced with complex passages containing sophisticated language, it is important for students to take a variety of steps before attempting to translate the text. We advocate for explicit instruction of these steps to mitigate common misconceptions.

- Students should read the sentence/paragraph carefully.
- Students should highlight or underline words/structures that they can translate immediately.
- Students should check the tense, the person, the verb ending, the adjectival endings, the gender of nouns, and whether they are singular or plural.
- For more complex sentences, students should break them down into smaller chunks or separate sentences.
- Students should translate each sentence individually, ensuring correct word order.
- Students should apply any necessary rules for connecting sentences (e.g. in German, when using subordinating conjunctions, placing the conjugated verb at the end; in Spanish, placing the adjective after the noun, etc.).
- When they encounter words for which they don't know the L2 equivalent, students should find suitable synonyms that do not alter the intended message; the message needs to be fully communicated, not literally!
- Students should fill in any gaps logically with words that make sense within the context (Bastow, 2021).

HACK #2

Tangled translation: Segments of the text requiring translation are presented in both L1 and L2. Students are directed to use one colour to highlight L1 text and another colour for L2 text. They subsequently undertake the task of translating or reconstructing the passages into both languages, on one side into L1 and on the other into L2.

HACK #3

Chain translation: Students work in pairs, with each pair receiving two A4 sheets in different colours, one with sentences in L2 to translate and the other with sentences in L1. Students alternate between translating into the L2 and L1. They begin by cutting the first sentence, translating it and then having their work checked by the teacher. This process continues, with students creating a chain of alternating colours as they progress. For different types of words, they could use different colours of paper.

 HACK #4

First letter translation: Students are given a text to translate into the L1, along with the first letters of each target language word, i.e. 'H..., i... h... B... u... i... h...'.

To reduce cognitive load, the activity can be presented as add below the task: Example in German:

My name is Kathrin. I have been playing the keyboard for five years. I play every day at home. I don't have favourite music, but I like pop music very much.			
I	h	K	I
s	s	f	J
K	l	s	j
T	z	H	I
h	k	L	a
i	m	P	s

 HACK #5

Folding translation: The teacher provides students with an A4 sheet containing sentences in the form of a list; sentences are spaced out. Students first translate the text into L1, then fold the sheet to hide L2 text and translate the L1 back into the L2. They unfold the paper to check their work, peeking as needed. The challenge is to unfold as little as possible, promoting active learning and retention.

 HACK #6

Mosaic translation: The teacher provides a task with a text in L1 that needs to be translated into L2. The teacher also supplies a grid containing words or chunks of the text already translated into L2. Students use these L2 words or chunks to translate and reconstruct the L1 text. They must apply their knowledge of grammar, including word order and syntax, to ensure the text is translated correctly.

HACK #7

Back-to-back translation: Students sit back-to-back, each with a text containing sentences in L1, and take turns to translate them into L2. The teacher circulates and listens to their translations. Alternatively, students could work in groups of three, with the third person acting as a referee who holds the correct L2 translation for the other two participants. Afterwards, students swap roles.

Conclusion

Various strategies can support students effectively in developing their translation skills. Further activities like bubble translation, honeycomb translation, rock climbing translation, jigsaw translation and text puzzle translation (Bastow, 2021) all offer similar scaffolding by providing target language chunks that students use to translate and reconstruct texts. While these activities support students by offering key language elements, they still present a challenge as students must apply their linguistic knowledge, including grammar and syntax, to reconstruct the text accurately. The MFL community is incredibly generous, with many colleagues sharing innovative and engaging activities that can make the process of translation both motivating and educational for students.

SECTION 3: FEEDBACK, ASSESSMENT AND REVISION

Feedback, assessment and revision are cornerstones of effective language learning in the context of MFL. Each of these elements plays a critical role in fostering a supportive learning environment, facilitating student progress, and ultimately leading to mastery of the TL.

Feedback

Feedback is an essential component of language learning, providing students with the information they need to improve and refine their skills. In MFL, feedback must be timely, specific and constructive. It helps students understand their errors, recognise areas where they need improvement and build on their strengths. Effective feedback goes beyond simple correction; it involves guiding students towards self-correction and encouraging them to reflect on their learning process. For example, when a student makes a grammatical mistake, rather than merely correcting it, a teacher might ask the student to identify the rule they missed and explain how to apply it correctly. This approach not only corrects the error but also reinforces the underlying grammatical concept, promoting deeper understanding and retention.

Assessment

Assessment, both formative and summative, is another critical aspect of MFL education.

- **Formative assessments**, such as retrieval quizzes, oral presentations (these could be recorded) and class activities, provide ongoing insights into student progress and understanding. These assessments enable teachers to identify gaps in knowledge and adapt their teaching accordingly. For instance, if a teacher notices that many students are struggling with a certain tense, they can revisit the concept, provide additional practice or employ different teaching strategies to address the issue.
- **Summative assessments**, such as end-of-term assessments or standardised tests, evaluate overall proficiency and comprehension. They provide a comprehensive overview of student learning and help teachers measure the effectiveness of their teaching approaches.

Revision

Revision supports effective language learning. Regular revision reinforces previously learned material, aids in the retention of vocabulary and grammar, and helps students build language skills and fluency. In the context of MFL, revision should be systematic and varied. This might include activities like spaced practice, where students review material at increasing intervals, or thematic revision sessions that focus on specific language skills such as listening, speaking, reading or writing. Incorporating revision into the daily or weekly routine ensures that language learning is continuous and cumulative, rather than a series of disjointed sessions.

CHAPTER 17
EFFECTIVE FEEDBACK IN MFL

Effective feedback in the MFL classroom is essential for guiding students towards language proficiency. More than merely correcting mistakes, feedback should nurture curiosity, encourage persistence and resilience, as well as help students understand their progress in a meaningful way. It's about creating an environment where students feel empowered to take risks and learn from their missteps. Here are five teaching hacks for giving feedback that resonates and inspires in the language classroom.

 HACK #1

Prioritise positivity with the 'compliment sandwich': The 'compliment sandwich' is a time-tested approach that balances constructive feedback with positivity. Begin by highlighting something the student did well; perhaps their pronunciation or effort in conjugating verbs correctly. Follow with an area for improvement, like sentence structure or verb agreement, and then finish with another positive note, such as their willingness to use new vocabulary. This method not only softens criticism but also boosts students' confidence, helping them see that every attempt moves them closer to fluency. It reminds them that language learning is a journey filled with wins and lessons.

 HACK #2

Use targeted language goals for precision: Feedback can often feel overwhelming, especially for younger or less-experienced learners. To keep it manageable, tie feedback to a specific goal for each lesson. For instance, if the focus is on pronunciation, let students know that feedback will mainly revolve around that area. This targeted approach helps students concentrate on one skill or element at a time and provides clear, actionable steps toward improvement. By knowing exactly where they stand with each goal, students can track their progress and develop confidence in specific language skills.

 HACK #3

Incorporate peer feedback for mutual growth: Peer feedback can be an empowering tool in language learning. Set up a feedback system where students pair up to review each other's work. Provide clear guidelines – such as identifying three strengths and one area for improvement. Peer feedback allows students to see how others approach the language, exposing them to different techniques and thought processes. It also fosters a supportive classroom culture where students feel like they're part of a learning community, learning from each other, and seeing how they're not alone in their language journey.

HACK #4

Use technology for immediate, private feedback: Technology can be an excellent resource for feedback in the language classroom. Tools like language apps, online quizzes or audio-recording platforms allow students to get instant feedback on pronunciation, spelling and grammar. Additionally, some tools enable students to work at their own pace, giving them time to absorb feedback without the immediate pressure of a live classroom. The private, personalised nature of tech feedback helps students process information without feeling self-conscious and lets them repeat tasks until they're satisfied with their performance.

HACK #5

Provide self-assessment tools to build autonomy: Encouraging students to reflect on their progress and self-assess can be one of the most effective forms of feedback. Create a checklist or rubric that students can use to evaluate their own work. For instance, if working on a written assignment, the checklist might include items like 'Did I use the correct tense?' or 'Did I incorporate at least three new vocabulary words?'. This method fosters independence and accountability. Students learn to see feedback not just as external critique but as an internal process, which can boost their self-confidence and make them more proactive in their language learning.

Conclusion

In the MFL classroom, feedback is more than a list of corrections; it's a vital tool for growth, self-reflection and encouragement. By using methods like the 'compliment sandwich', targeted goals, peer feedback, technology and self-assessment, teachers can create a nurturing environment where students feel safe to take risks and grow. This approach to feedback not only builds language skills but also nurtures students' resilience, curiosity and love for learning. It can support their development in other subjects too!

CHAPTER 18
METACOGNITION: PREPARING FOR ASSESSMENTS

> Ms Johnson stands at the front of the classroom, her disappointment evident as she glances over the faces of her students. Today is supposed to be the long-anticipated day of the final assessment; a culmination of weeks of hard work and preparation. Yet, as she hands out the papers, one by one, she notices the telltale signs of unreadiness: the furrowed brows, the hesitant scribbling, the occasional frustrated sighs, the fidgeting and looking around. It's evident that some of her students have not taken the time to study or organise themselves sufficiently to prepare for the assessment.
>
> Glancing around the room, she notices a few students struggling to even begin the tasks. It's clear that their lack of preparation is hindering their ability to perform well on the assessment.
>
> As the papers begin to pile up on her desk, with some containing barely a few lines, Ms Johnson can't help but feel a sense of disappointment wash over her. She has spent countless hours preparing engaging lessons, providing extra resources and homework materials, and offering intervention support to ensure her students are ready for this moment. But it seems that her efforts have fallen short for some.
>
> Despite her disappointment, Ms Johnson makes a mental note to address the issue with her students, emphasising the importance of self-organisation, planning, effective studying and preparing for future assessments.

Considering the potential lack of preparation and self-organisation among Ms Johnson's students for this assessment, it becomes clear that fostering metacognitive strategies within our classrooms and teaching students how to self-regulate is essential for their success, self-belief and academic growth. For instance, by prompting students to set specific and attainable study goals, consistently monitor their progress and evaluate the effectiveness of their study habits – as could have been advantageous for Ms Johnson's class – we can improve their capability to prepare for assessments effectively.

What is self-regulation and metacognition?

Self-regulated learning can be divided into three fundamental components that teachers should be aware of to assist their students in becoming successful learners: cognition, metacognition and motivation (EEF, 2018).

Cognition

Cognition involves the mental processes or actions involved in acquiring knowledge or understanding through thoughts, experiences and senses. In MFL classrooms, cognitive strategies may include methods such as memorisation techniques for learning vocabulary or grammar concepts. Some useful techniques include mnemonics like AVOCADO (Adjectives, Verbs, Opinions, Connectives, Adverbs, Descriptions, Other) and PALMW, incorporating songs, tunes and rhythms, and teaching word families.

Metacognition

Metacognition, often defined as 'thinking about thinking' or the ability to reflect on and regulate one's own thinking processes, can empower students to become more self-aware and effective as learners. It involves the methods learners employ to monitor and intentionally guide their learning. For instance, after choosing a specific cognitive strategy for vocabulary memorisation, such as self-quizzing, a student can then assess its effectiveness and consciously adjust their strategy based on the outcome. Metacognitive strategies refer to the techniques used to oversee or regulate our cognition, such as verifying the accuracy of our memorisation method or selecting the most suitable cognitive strategy for the given task.

By teaching metacognitive strategies – such as goal setting, planning and organising, monitoring and evaluating (self-reflection, self-questioning) – teachers can help students take ownership of their learning journey. True metacognition involves a range of behaviours that are sustained over a period of time. This takes preparation and practice.

Motivation

Motivation relates to students' readiness to employ their metacognitive and cognitive abilities in the learning process. Motivational approaches may entail persuading oneself to tackle a challenging revision task immediately, impacting their present state of wellbeing, as a means of enhancing their future wellbeing for the upcoming test.

Why is metacognition important?

Studies suggest that engaging in metacognition enhances learning outcomes, potentially resulting in 7 additional months of progress (EEF, 2018). It helps to shape active rather than passive learners, provides learners with a sense of control over their learning, makes students aware of their own thinking, and promotes 'deep learning'. Through metacognition, they understand themselves as learners. They understand the task at hand as well as a variety of strategies and how to use them in a variety of situations.

Here are some examples of metacognitive strategies for the MFL classroom:

HACK #1

'Thinking out loud': This involves physically engaging with the activity, modelling metacognitive questioning by talking through the task.

- Modelling the process of approaching the task:
    - Highlighting connections to previous topics, vocabulary and structures.
    - Annotating the task.
    - Understanding the process; fostering self-efficacy.
    - Proof checking the work.
- Modelling metacognitive regulation before, during and after the task:
    - Before the task – planning the approach. What is the task asking me to do? Have I done this type of task before?
    - During the task – monitoring the progress. What strategies/methods can I use? Am I being effective?
    - After the task – evaluating the performance. Have I succeeded? How do I know? What do I need to do next time? How can I improve?

HACK #2

Self-assessment checklist: By going through this type of checklist, students can assess their performance objectively and identify areas where they can develop their skills and knowledge further. Instructions for the student:

- **Set aside time**: Find a quiet space where you can focus without distraction.
- **Clarity of goals**: Did you clearly define what you wanted to achieve?
- **Understanding of tasks**: Did you understand what was required of you for each task?
- **Time management**: Did you manage your time effectively to complete the tasks on time?
- **Quality of work**: Is your work accurate, thorough and well-presented?

- **Problem-solving (vocabulary, concepts, rules)**: Were you able to overcome any challenges or obstacles encountered during the tasks?
- **Reflection**: Have you reflected on your work and identified areas for improvement?
- **Feedback incorporation**: Have you considered previous feedback from teachers or peers and used it to improve your work?
- **Self-motivation**: Did you stay motivated and focused throughout the tasks?

HACK #3

DIRT: 'Dedicated improvement and reflection time' is a period in the classroom that is designated for students to reflect on their learning, receive feedback and set goals for improvement. This practice encourages critical thinking about their progress, helping students identify areas where they need additional support or clarification. Engaging in DIRT allows students to take ownership of their learning and develop essential self-regulation skills for lifelong learning. Teachers who incorporate reflection time into their lessons can foster self-awareness, motivation and independence in their students, leading to improved academic outcomes.

Reflection worksheet

Name: _____

Date: _____

1. Checklist

Criterion	Yes	No	Comments
Correct use of verb tenses			
Proper agreement of nouns/adjectives			
Variety and appropriateness of vocabulary			
Use of connectors and conjunctions			
Accuracy in sentence structure			

2. Highlight and reflect

Strengths

Example 1: _____

Example 2: _____

Areas for improvement

Example 1: _____

Example 2: _____

3. Peer feedback

Partner's name: _____

Feedback received: _____

4. Improvement goals

Goal 1: _____

Goal 2: _____

Actions to achieve goals: _____

5. Reflection

What I learned from this activity: _____

How I plan to apply my goals in future tasks: _____

 HACK #4

Personal learning checklist: This tool contains a comprehensive list of required learning objectives for a unit or course. Students review each topic on the list, marking their confidence and the security of their understanding for each item.

Personal learning checklists exemplify self-regulated learning and metacognition, as they enable students to monitor, evaluate and plan their learning effectively. By using them, students can take control of their educational progress and make informed decisions about where to focus their efforts.

HACK #5

Study timetable: Following on from Hack #4, using a study timetable can help support students with their self-regulation and time management in a smart way so they can do their best in all elements of language learning. With a timetable, they can plan what and when to study and revise. Explicitly teach and advise students on:

- **Planning their schedule**: Set aside time slots for each subject, homework and breaks.
- **Prioritising tasks**: Decide which subjects or assignments need more attention and allocate more time to them.
- **Staying consistent**: Students should stick to their timetable to build a regular study routine.
- **Including breaks**: Remind students to schedule short breaks to rest and recharge between study sessions.
- **Balancing their time**: Make sure to include time for other activities like hobbies, sports or spending time with family and friends.
- **Staying flexible**: Students should adjust their timetable as needed if something unexpected comes up or if they find a better way to manage their time.
- **Reviewing and adjusting**: Regularly review their timetable to see what's working and what isn't and adjust accordingly.

German revision timetable for GCSE exam

Week number	Date (week beginning)	Topics	Role play	Picture card	Questions completed	Revision resource made	Carousel	Workbook pages	Signed parent/guardian
1	18/9/23	World of work	9		1–3				
2	25/9/23	World of work		7	4–5				
3	2/10/23	World of work	10		6–8				
4	9/10/23	World of work		8	9–10				
5	16/10/23	Global and international dimension	1		1–3				
6	23/10/23	Global and international dimension		2	4–5				
7	6/11/23	Global and international dimension	9		6–7				
8	13/11/23	Global and international dimension		10	8–9				
9	20/11/23	Global and international dimension		6	10				
10	27/11/23	School life	8		1–3				
11	4/12/23	School life		5	4–6				
12	11/12/23	School life	7		7–10				
13	18/12/23	Identity and culture	2		1–3				
14	1/1/24	Identity and culture		1	4–6				
15	8/1/24	Identity and culture	3		7–10				
16	15/1/24	Identity and culture		4	11–14				
17	22/1/24	Local area, holiday, travel	4		1–3				
18	29/1/24	Local area, holiday, travel		3	4–6				
19	5/2/24	Local area, holiday, travel	5		7–10				
20	12/2/24	Local area, holiday, travel	6		11–14				

🔒 MORE HACKS

In the subsequent revision chapter, you may find further suggestions for metacognitive strategies worth exploring.

Conclusion

Metacognitive strategies offer a powerful framework for enhancing learning outcomes and fostering deeper understanding. Embracing a metacognitive approach can greatly benefit both teachers and students in maximising their potential. While some students may naturally exhibit metacognitive thinking, its development is significantly influenced by adult guidance, especially during the formative years. However, without explicit instruction in the classroom, this skill may diminish over time. Therefore, fostering self-regulated learning within educational settings is crucial for nurturing metacognitive abilities and promoting academic success.

CHAPTER 19
REVISION STRATEGIES

> Maya sits at her desk, surrounded by stacks of textbooks and piles of notes. Despite spending hours revising, she feels totally lost, like she's just wasting time. It feels as though the knowledge is not sticking in her brain at all. Each study session feels like a battle. Maya tries to make sense of her notes and the vast amount of vocabulary, but they all seem to blur into an incomprehensible mess. The more she tries to focus, the more her mind wanders, leaving her feeling defeated and demoralised.
>
> Maya has talked with her friends about revision and tried various revision techniques – from highlighting to rereading the notes and vocabulary in her exercise book – but nothing seems to stick. It's as if she's spinning her wheels, using up all her energy, without making any progress. With each passing day, Maya gets more and more stressed and anxious. The weight of looming exams hangs heavy on her shoulders, and she worries that she'll fail and disappoint her parents and teacher.
>
> She starts exploring new study strategies, seeking advice from her teachers and classmates, and experimenting with different approaches hoping to find one that will work for her.

We frequently give our students homework assignments aimed at revision, but do they truly understand what revision really means? Revision is more than just rereading notes, highlighting or mechanic memorising of vocabulary; it involves a deeper engagement with the language and its application. Maya's situation, where she struggles to make sense of her notes and vocabulary, prompts us to wonder whether our students possess the essential knowledge and skills for effective revision. Are they equipped with strategies for organising information, applying key concepts in context, and making meaningful connections between them? Maya's challenges highlight the need for us to assess and teach these crucial revision techniques, ensuring that our students can approach their studies with confidence and clarity.

Revision is a critical aspect of the learning process, yet many students struggle to employ effective strategies, often opting for methods that are easier but less impactful. As teachers, we frequently observe students using ineffective revision techniques, such as passive rereading of their vocabulary (notes) or highlighting, which may provide a false sense of productivity but do little to enhance long-term retention, application and understanding. It is essential for students to recognise the importance of employing high-impact revision strategies that maximise their learning outcomes.

It refers to the process of reviewing, re-examining and actively recalling material that has been previously studied, typically in preparation for an exam or assessment. It involves actively 'going over' course materials, such as vocabulary and language structures, with the aim of reinforcing learning and clarifying understanding, as well as improving language skills and the retention of key concepts which can be achieved through extensive practice and processing.

One reason why students may gravitate towards ineffective revision techniques is their perceived ease and familiarity. Passive activities, like rereading notes or textbooks, require minimal effort and can create a sense of accomplishment without necessarily leading to deeper learning or retention. Additionally, students may rely on these strategies because they have been widely used in the past or because they are encouraged by their peers, without considering their effectiveness in promoting meaningful learning.

However, it is essential for our students to understand that not all revision strategies are created equal. High-impact revision techniques are those that actively engage learners and promote deep processing of vocabulary and structures.

Where to start?

Before students begin their revision, it is essential they consider the following things that all students should do:

- **Identify what they already know** (strengths) and stop relearning it. While it might feel satisfying to confirm their existing knowledge, it is not productive.
- **Determine what they don't know** (weaknesses) and focus their efforts there.
- **Assess their knowledge level** and choose the appropriate strategy to address their knowledge gaps.
- **Repeat the process**, gradually narrowing down the material they need to learn at each stage.
- **Plan their revision** and set achievable targets.
- **Consider studying with a friend** and, if possible, having a 'study buddy'.

 HACK #1

Retrieval practice: To implement this low-effort, high-impact strategy of practice testing effectively, students could follow these instructions:

- **Active retrieval through low-stakes quizzes**: Engage in practice testing by actively recalling information from memory through quizzes. This process enhances long-term retention and comprehension compared to passive review methods.
- **Incorporate spaced repetition**: Space out their study sessions over time to reinforce learning and prevent forgetting. Review material strategically at spaced intervals, strengthening memory and retention of key concepts.
- **Avoid massed practice**: Steer clear of cramming information all at once, as it leads to short-term retention but limited long-term recall. Instead, opt for spaced repetition to enhance memory retention.
- **Apply interleaved practice**: Mix different topics or types of problems within a study session, such as grammatical concepts like tenses, rather than focusing on one concept at a time. This technique challenges students to actively switch between concepts, improving long-term retention and discrimination between different types of information.

HACK #2

Self-quizzing: This is an effective technique for reinforcing language learning and enhancing long-term retention of new words. To self-quiz, or effectively learn chunks of vocabulary using spaced repetition and interleaved practice, students could follow these steps:

- **Identify the chunks**: Choose no more than 3–5 chunks of vocabulary you want to learn. This could be words, phrases or expressions that you need to remember.
- **Read and repeat**: Spend 5–10 minutes reading and repeating each chunk of vocabulary, preferably aloud. Focus on pronunciation and understanding the meaning of each chunk.
- **Cover and recall**: Once you have learned the chunks, cover them with your hand or a sheet of paper. Try to recall each chunk from memory without looking. Don't rush your answers. Correct and mark each chunk with a tick or a cross based on whether you recalled it correctly.
- **Review incorrect answers**: Check the correct answers for the chunks you got wrong. Repeat the process with the incorrect chunks until you have learned them accurately.
- **Interleave and space out learning**: Mix in new chunks with the ones you have already learned. Space out your learning sessions over time to reinforce memory and prevent forgetting. Break down your study sessions into manageable 20-minute sessions for regular practice.

Chapter 19 REVISION STRATEGIES

Self-quizzing Knowledge Organiser (KO)

1. Identify	2. Learn	3. Cover
Have a pen and paper ready. Use your KO to identify the knowledge or chunks you want to learn.	Choose no more than 5 chunks and spend 5–10 minutes actively reading and repeating them in your head or aloud.	After you have learned the chunks, cover them with your hand or a sheet of paper.
4. Write 	5. Correct 	6. Repeat
Think hard and write the chunks on the sheet of paper from memory. Don't rush your answers.	Correct and mark each chunk/word in red pen, putting a tick or a cross by each word/answer. Check correct answers.	Repeat the process with the chunks you have got wrong and add new chunks (maximum of 5 at a time) until you have learned them.

Interleave and space out your learning; break it down into shorter, regular sessions (20–30 mins) to ensure you retain the knowledge for longer.

A strategy for self-quizzing. Idea for visual by S Bastow.

HACK #3

The Leitner system: To effectively use the Leitner system for learning vocabulary, students could follow these steps:

- **Start with sorting**: Arrange your flashcards into different boxes based on your familiarity with each card's content. Begin with all cards in the first box.
- **Daily review of Box 1**: During your study sessions, review the flashcards in the first box daily. Test your memory by recalling the information on each card. If you answer correctly, move the card to the next box.
- **Gradually spaced repetition**: Increase the intervals between reviews as you progress through the boxes. For example, cards in Box 2 might be reviewed every two days, those in Box 3 every four days, and so on. This spaced repetition strengthens memory retention.
- **Move back for review**: If you struggle to recall information on a card during review, move it back to the first box for more frequent practice.

- **Optimise study time**: Spend more time on difficult cards and less on those you already know well. This structured approach optimises your study time and reinforces memory efficiently.
- **Leverage the spacing effect**: Gradually increasing the intervals between reviews for well-known cards leverages the spacing effect, enhancing long-term retention.

Additionally, consider the format of the flashcards. While digital platforms offer convenience, many students still prefer physical flashcards for tactile learning. Practising with a partner in the classroom or having a 'study buddy' can also enhance learning through collaborative work.

Using flashcards: the Leitner system

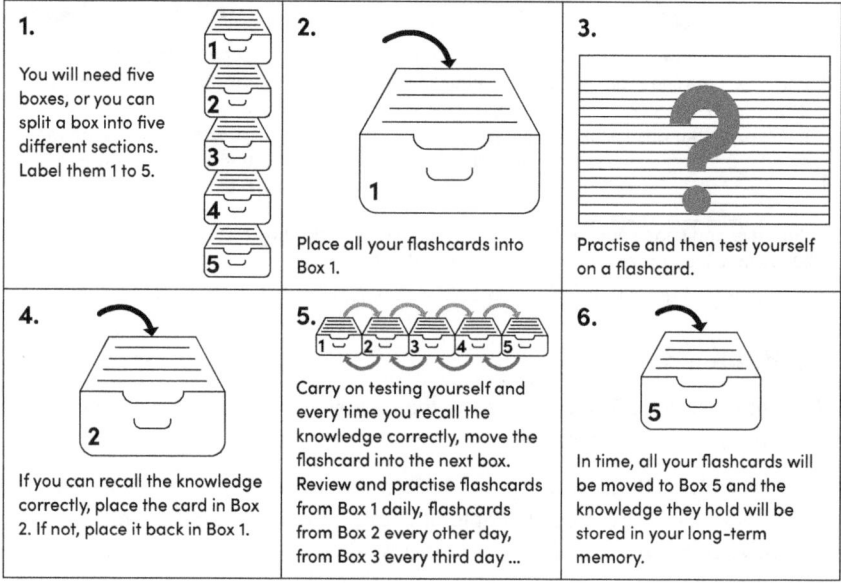

The Leitner system of revision for learning and retaining vocabulary. Idea for visual by S Bastow.

 HACK #4

Mind maps: To use mind maps effectively for revision (speaking and writing), teachers and students could follow these steps:

- **Topic**: Select a topic related to the content you want to revise. This could be a specific language skill (e.g. vocabulary, grammar) or a broader topic (e.g. travel, food, culture).

- **Central point**: Write down the main theme in the centre of a blank page. This serves as the principal focus of the mind map.
- **Branches**: Identify the main concepts or subtopics related to the central theme. Create branches radiating from the central point and label each branch with a main concept (nouns, verbs, adjectives, etc.).
- **Details and associations**: For each main concept, add further details, keywords or related terms. Use short phrases, keywords or images to represent each idea. Connect these details to the corresponding main concept using smaller branches.
- **Visual cues**: Incorporate visual cues such as colours, symbols and icons to enhance the visual appeal and organisation of the mind map. Use different colours for different categories or themes to aid memory recall.
- **Examples and context**: Provide examples or context for each concept to reinforce understanding and aid memory retention. Use arrows or lines to indicate relationships between concepts and examples.
- **Review and refine**: Review the mind map and ensure that all relevant information is included. Adjust as needed to clarify connections or add additional details.
- **Test your understanding**: Use the mind map as a revision tool to test the content. Cover sections of the mind map and try to recall the information associated with each concept.

Conclusion

While it may be tempting for students to rely on familiar but ineffective revision strategies, it is essential for them to recognise the importance of employing high-impact techniques that promote meaningful learning. By employing a combination of strategies, such as practice testing, spaced repetition, interleaved practice and visual aids like mind maps, students can optimise their study sessions and enhance their long-term memory recall. Consistent and deliberate practice, coupled with strategic review techniques, not only improves performance in assessments but also fosters a deeper mastery of the subject. Ultimately, embracing these effective revision strategies empowers learners to achieve their academic goals and cultivate a lifelong love for learning. As teachers, it is our responsibility to guide students towards these effective strategies and empower them to take control of their own learning journey.

SECTION 4: TECHNOLOGY INTEGRATION

Incorporating technology into MFL teaching not only transforms the learning experience but also addresses the evolving needs of twenty-first-century learners.

By leveraging digital tools and platforms, teachers can create a more dynamic and interactive classroom environment where students are actively engaged in their language-learning journey.

Language-learning apps and online resources offer students the flexibility to practise vocabulary, grammar and pronunciation at their own pace, catering to individual learning preferences and schedules.

Moreover, the integration of multimedia content such as videos, podcasts and interactive games not only captivates students' attention but also provides authentic cultural contexts for language usage. Virtual reality (VR) technology further enhances this immersion by transporting students to virtual language environments, allowing them to experience real-life situations without leaving the classroom.

Additionally, technology facilitates instant feedback through automated assessment systems and peer collaboration tools, enabling students to receive timely guidance and support. By embracing technology, MFL teachers can empower students to become more autonomous, resourceful and globally connected learners, preparing them to thrive in an increasingly interconnected world.

CHAPTER 20
EFFECTIVE USE OF TECHNOLOGY TO ENHANCE LEARNING

Integrating technology into the MFL classroom has transformed the way students engage with language learning. Beyond digital convenience, effective use of technology offers students immersive, interactive and personalised experiences that deepen their understanding and spark enthusiasm. For today's students, technology in the language classroom can make the language they're studying feel alive and relevant to the real world. Here are five teaching hacks to maximise the impact of technology on language learning and create a dynamic classroom environment, leaning into the benefits of technology rather than the difficulties it can often present.

HACK #1

Virtual pen pals for real-world communication: One of the most powerful ways to bring a language to life is to connect students with native speakers through virtual pen-pal exchanges. Platforms like ePals or Padlet allow students to engage with peers from different countries, practising real-world communication in the target language. For example, students studying French could partner with students in a French-speaking region, exchanging messages, cultural insights or even video diaries. This interaction helps students gain confidence, learn authentic expressions and experience cultural diversity first hand. Virtual exchanges make language learning not only an academic endeavour but also a meaningful, human experience.

HACK #2

Digital flashcards for vocabulary retention: Building vocabulary is key in language acquisition, and digital flashcard apps like Quizlet and Anki offer engaging ways for students to practise new words. Encourage students to create their own flashcards based on each week's vocabulary list. These platforms often use spaced repetition, so words students find challenging will appear more frequently, reinforcing memory retention. For fun, create flashcard challenges in class where students test each other, or host small competitions. The advantage of digital flashcards lies in their accessibility; students can practise on the go, turning short moments of downtime into productive language-learning opportunities.

HACK #3

Voice recording for pronunciation practice: In the MFL classroom, mastering pronunciation can be challenging. Voice-recording apps like Speechling or Vocaroo allow students to record and listen to themselves speaking in the target language, encouraging self-awareness and progress over time. Give students pronunciation tasks, such as reading a short passage aloud or practising key phrases. They can then listen back, self-assess and even receive feedback from peers or teachers. Voice recording helps students build confidence and refine their speaking skills in a non-intimidating, reflective manner, making pronunciation practice a positive part of their routine.

HACK #4

Gamification for motivation and engagement: Bringing elements of gamification into the MFL classroom can create a fun, competitive spirit that motivates students. Apps like Duolingo and Kahoot! turn language practice into a game, complete with points, levels and rewards. Use these apps as warm-up activities, homework or even as part of in-class competitions. Create weekly leaderboards or award small prizes for top scorers to encourage friendly competition. Gamification not only motivates students but also keeps them engaged, making practice feel like play rather than work.

HACK #5

Virtual field trips for cultural immersion: Technology has opened the door to virtual field trips, allowing students to explore cultural landmarks and iconic sites from the classroom. Websites like Google Earth, virtual museum tours or language-specific YouTube channels let students experience places like the Louvre in Paris, the streets of Barcelona or even ancient ruins in Rome. Design a lesson where students 'visit' these places, guiding them through activities that explore the history, art and culture of the target-language country. Virtual field trips create memorable experiences, connecting students' language skills to a broader cultural context and fostering a deeper appreciation of the world beyond their own.

FURTHER HACKS FROM EDTECH MFL EXPERT JÉRÔME NOGUES

Technology in language teaching can be both a blessing and a curse. As someone who's spent years immersed in EdTech and guiding teachers through the digital landscape, I've seen it all: the good, the bad and the 'why did we even try that?'.

Before we dive into the coolest tech tools for language classrooms, let's set one thing straight: only use tech if it genuinely enhances your teaching. Sounds obvious, right? Yet, it's easy to get dazzled by the latest shiny app or AI tool, only to discover it complicates rather than simplifies.

So, let's explore how we can actually use technology to elevate our language teaching. When applied well, it's transformative.

Engaging vocabulary with retrieval practice

Starting or ending a lesson with quick, effective retrieval practice is key to solidifying vocabulary. Certain apps make this a breeze. With interactive tools that gamify vocabulary, students are not only reviewing but actively recalling terms, which strengthens long-term memory. Apps like Quizlet or Kahoot! offer customisable games and quizzes that turn vocabulary learning into an engaging competition. These apps let students revisit key terms in a low-stakes, enjoyable way, giving teachers instant insights into which words need extra attention.

Listening

Remember those clunky language-lab cassettes? (If you're too young to remember cassettes, count yourself lucky!) Today, teachers can use AI tools that customise listening exercises to each student's level, authentic podcasts from around the world, and tools that break down rapid native speech into manageable chunks or create automatic subtitles. This is a total game-changer.

Speaking

Speaking practice has had a major upgrade, too. We all know how nerve-wracking it is for students to speak a new language in front of the class. Here's where tech becomes a lifesaver. AI conversation partners, like ChatGPT or chatbots created in Mizou, give students a safe space to practise, reducing 'mind-blank' moments in front of their peers. Speech-analysis tools also let them perfect their pronunciation, as if they had a patient native speaker on call. Furthermore, voice typing on various platforms can also be fun to use to work on phonics and, of course, really useful for pupils with learning difficulties.

Reading

When it comes to reading, it's not just PDFs of textbook pages anymore. Today's tools can adapt complex articles to match each student's level without diluting content. Think of it as having a smart teaching assistant who tailors any text to be just the right level of challenge. Moreover, tools like the mighty accessibility tool Immersive Reader can be extremely useful to help comprehension for all.

Writing

And what about writing? It's come a long way from red-pen corrections. AI writing assistants act like knowledgeable friends, gently steering students back on track. However, one has to be careful here; AI education and ethics are needed. The tools are here to help not to do the job for you! Each school needs to have a policy in place to avoid mishaps.

In my opinion, the real magic happens when students collaborate on projects with peers from other countries. Suddenly, a language essay isn't just homework – it's a chance to build cross-cultural connections.

What I've learned from experimenting with classroom tech

The best technology is like a great referee – it's doing its job best when you barely notice it's there. Just as a good ref keeps the game flowing smoothly without stealing the spotlight, effective tech should quietly facilitate language learning without drawing attention to itself. When students are so immersed in using the language that they forget the tech, that's when you know you've hit the sweet spot.

The bottom line

Technology isn't here to replace teachers. It's here to make our lives easier and our teaching more impactful. Use it purposefully, and it's like having a super-powered teaching assistant. Use it just because it's there, and … well, we've all been there.

Remember, it's not about having the fanciest tech setup or the latest apps. It's about finding tools that genuinely support your students' learning. Keep that in mind, and you're golden!

Conclusion

Effective use of technology in the MFL classroom transforms language learning into an interactive, enjoyable and meaningful experience. By integrating some of the tools above, and with the advice of Jérôme, teachers can create a dynamic environment that encourages students to engage with the language in a genuine way. These methods not only enhance language acquisition but also build confidence, cultural understanding and enthusiasm for exploring new worlds through language. The MFL classroom becomes a gateway to connection and curiosity, and technology is the bridge that helps us get there.

CONCLUSION

This book has been written with the aim of equipping you, the MFL teacher, with a range of practical strategies, or hacks, to address some of the most challenging aspects of language teaching. We recognise that teaching a second language, especially within the constraints of a typical classroom setting, presents its own unique difficulties – from mastering grammar, vocabulary and communicative skills to fostering cultural understanding. The ideas and strategies outlined in each chapter were designed to support you in addressing these complexities in ways that are adaptable to your various teaching contexts and student needs.

Rather than advocating for a one-size-fits-all solution or promoting a singular pedagogical approach, this book has sought to highlight the importance of flexibility, adaptability and professional judgement in the classroom. We do not claim to provide a silver bullet for the challenges of language teaching. Instead, we would like to encourage you to view the suggested 'hacks' as a toolkit – something you can dip into as needed, adapting or amending strategies based on the context of your classroom and the learners in front of you.

We believe that the teachers themselves, with their first-hand knowledge of their students, are in the best position to decide which strategies will work in their specific setting. Whether you are a newly qualified teacher or an experienced educator, the hacks outlined in this book are intended to be flexible, allowing for creativity and experimentation. We hope that by offering a range of ideas and approaches, you will be able to choose and modify strategies that resonate with your teaching style and curriculum goals. Some ideas may resonate more than others, and we hope that you will feel empowered to try, adjust or even ignore certain approaches based on what you know will best serve your students' progress.

Furthermore, this book recognises the limitations of classroom time and acknowledges that replicating natural language acquisition processes, like those of a first language, is not always feasible. Instead, we have explored how explicit instruction, when thoughtfully applied, can complement natural language learning in a structured, school-based environment. We hope you enjoy reading it and are looking forward to your feedback.

KEY TERMS

A-level	Advanced level
AQA	Exam board (England)
CI	Comprehensible input
CLT	Communicative language teaching
CPD	Continuous professional development
DfE	Department for Education
DIRT	Dedicated improvement and reflection time
Edexcel	Exam board (England)
EEF	Education Endowment Foundation
EPI	Extensive processing instruction
GCSE	General Certificate in Secondary Education
GILT	Global Innovative Language Teachers
KO	Knowledge organisers
KS	Key stage
L1	First language
L2	Second language
LDP	Language driven pedagogy
MFL	Modern foreign languages
NCELP	National Centre for Excellence for Language Pedagogy
SLA	Second language acquisition
SSC	Sound-spelling correspondences
T&L	Teaching and learning
TL	Target language
TPRS	Teaching Proficiency through Reading and Storytelling
VR	Virtual reality
WAGOLL	What a Good One Looks Like

BIBLIOGRAPHY

AQA (2024). Specification 'GCSE Spanish (8692)'. Available at: www.aqa.org.uk/subjects/spanish/gcse/spanish-8692/specification

Avery, N., Kasprowicz, R., Norris, J.M. & Ortega, L. (2019). 'What do 49 studies tell us about the effectiveness of grammar teaching?' *OASIS Summary* of Norris & Ortega (2001) in *Language Learning*. Available at: www.oasis-database.org/details/rx913p922

Barcroft, J. (2019). 'Issues in learning single words'. In S. Webb (Ed.), *The Routledge Handbook of Vocabulary Studies* (pp.479–492). New York: Routledge. Available at: https://sites.wustl.edu/barcroft/publications/

Bastow, S. (2021). 'Translation – tangled, rock climbing, bubble, mosaic, ping-pong ...'. FrauBastowMFL (Blog) 1 January. Available at: www.fraubastowmfl.co.uk/post/translation-tangled-rock-climbing-bubble-mosaic-ping-pong-1

Bauckham, I. (2016). 'Modern Foreign Languages Pedagogy Review: A review of modern foreign languages teaching practice in Key Stage 3 and Key Stage 4'. Teaching Schools Council. Available at: https://ncelp.org/wp-content/uploads/2020/02/MFL_Pedagogy_Review_Report_TSC_PUBLISHED_VERSION_Nov_2016_1_.pdf

Conti, G. (2018). 'Patterns first – how I teach lexicogrammar (Part 1)'. The Language Gym (Blog) 30 July. Available at: https://gianfrancoconti.com/2018/07/30/patterns-first-how-i-teach-lexicogrammar-part-1/

Conti, G. (2020a). 'The art and science of creating sentence builders – key factors to consider in creating your sentence builders'. The Language Gym (Blog) 4 May. Available at: https://gianfrancoconti.com/2020/05/04/the-art-and-science-of-creating-sentence-builders-key-factors-to-consider-in-creating-your-sentence-builder/

Conti, G. (2020b). 'My approach: Extensive Processing Instruction (E.P.I.) – an important clarification in response to many queries'. The Language Gym (Blog) 9 January. Available at: https://gianfrancoconti.com/2020/01/09/my-approach-extensive-processing-instruction-e-p-i-an-important-clarification-in-response-to-many-queries/

Department for Education (2022). 'GCSE French, German and Spanish subject content: Subject content aims and learning objectives for French, German and Spanish GCSEs from 2024'. Available at: www.gov.uk/government/publications/gcse-french-german-and-spanish-subject-content

Education Endowment Foundation (2018). 'Metacognition and self-regulated learning: Guidance report'. Available at: https://educationendowmentfoundation.org.uk/education-evidence/guidance-reports/metacognition

Erler, L. & Macaro, E. (2011). 'Decoding ability in French as a foreign language and language learning motivation'. *Modern Language Journal*, 95(4): 496–518. Available at: https://doi.org/10.1111/j.1540-4781.2011.01238.x

Graham, S. (2017). 'Research into practice: Listening strategies in an instructed classroom setting'. *Language Teaching*, 50(1): 107–119.

Hamada, M. & Koda, K. (2008). 'Influence of first language orthographic experience on second language decoding and word learning'. *Language Learning*, 58(1): 1–31. Available at: https://doi.org/10.1111/j.1467-9922.2007.00433.x

Kasprowicz, R.E. & Marsden, E. (2018). 'Teaching grammar through different types of input activities'. *OASIS Summary* of Kasprowicz & Marsden (2018) in *Applied Linguistics*. Available at: www.oasis-database.org/details/m039k4882

Macaro, E. (2007). 'Do near-beginner learners of French have any writing strategies?' *The Language Learning Journal*, 35(1): 23–35. Available at: https://doi.org/10.1080/09571730701315600

Milton, J. (2009). *Measuring Second Language Vocabulary Acquisition*. Second Language Acquisition: 45. Series editor: David Singleton. Trinity College. Dublin. Ireland. p.58.

Milton, J. (2013). *Measuring the contribution of vocabulary knowledge to proficiency in the four skills*. (PDF) EUROSLA Monographs Series 2. p.71.

Müller, L-M., Spada, N. & Tomita, Y. (2018). 'The relationship between the type of teaching and simple and complex grammatical features'. *OASIS Summary* of Spada & Tomita (2010) in *Language Learning*. www.oasis-database.org/details/qn59q3974

Myatt, M. & Tomsett, J. (2021*). Huh: Curriculum conversations between subject and curriculum leaders*. Woodbridge: John Catt Educational Ltd.

Nassaji, H. (2003). 'L2 vocabulary learning from context: strategies, knowledge sources, and their relationship with success in L2 lexical inferencing'. *TESOL Quarterly*, 37(4): 645–70. Available at: https://doi.org/10.2307/3588216

Nation, I.S.P. (2001). *Learning Vocabulary in Another Language*. (1st edn.). Cambridge: Cambridge University Press.

Nation, I.S.P. (2007). 'The four strands'. *Innovation in Language Learning and Teaching*, 1(1): 2–13. Available at: https://doi.org/10.2167/illt039.0

Nation, I.S.P. (2013). *Learning Vocabulary in Another Language (Cambridge Applied Linguistics)* (2nd edn.). Cambridge: Cambridge University Press.

Ofsted (2021). 'Research review series: languages'. Available at: www.gov.uk/government/publications/curriculum-research-review-series-languages

Pearson Education (2016). 'GCSE (9–1) German specification'. Available at: https://qualifications.pearson.com/en/qualifications/edexcel-gcses/german-2016.html

Pearson Education (2024). 'GCSE (9–1) German specification'. Available at: https://qualifications.pearson.com/content/dam/pdf/GCSE/German/2024/specification-and-sample-assessments/gcse-9-1-german-specification.pdf

Printer, L. (2019). 'Student perceptions on the motivational pull of Teaching Proficiency through Reading and Storytelling (TPRS): a self-determination theory perspective'. *The Language Learning Journal*, 49(3): 288–301. Available at: https://doi.org/10.1080/09571736.2019.1566397

Sardinha, T.B. (2019). 'Lexicogrammar'. *The Encyclopedia of Applied Linguistics*. Wiley Online Library. Available at: https://doi.org/10.1002/9781405198431.wbeal0698.pub2

Schmitt, N. (2008). 'Review article: Instructed second language vocabulary learning'. *Language Teaching Research*, 12(3): 329–363. Available at: https://doi.org/10.1177/1362168808089921

University of York (n.d.). MultilingProfiler. Available at: www.multilingprofiler.net/

Wajnryb, R. (1990). *Grammar dictation*. Oxford: Oxford University Press.

Warren, D. (2018). 'GCSE writing preparation'. Morgan MFL (Blog) 21 January. Available at: https://morganmfl.weebly.com/blog/gcse-writing-preparation

Warren, D. (2019). *100 Ideas for Secondary Teachers: Outstanding MFL lessons*. London: Bloomsbury.

Woore, R. (2009). 'Beginners' progress in decoding L2 French: some longitudinal evidence from English modern foreign languages classrooms'. *The Language Learning Journal*, 37(1): 3–18. Available at: https://doi.org/10.1080/09571730902717398

Woore, R. (2022). 'What can second language acquisition research tell us about the phonics "pillar"?'. *The Language Learning Journal*, 50(2): 172–185. Available at: https://doi.org/10.1080/09571736.2022.2045683

Zhang, T. (2023). 'Grammar instruction in communicative language teaching: balancing fluency and accuracy for language proficiency'. *Journal of Education Humanities and Social Sciences*, 23: 715–719. Available at: www.researchgate.net/publication/376980560_Grammar_Instruction_in_Communicative_Language_Teaching_Balancing_Fluency_and_Accuracy_for_Language_Proficiency

Personalised professional development from Hachette Learning Academy

A simple way to boost career progression, staff motivation and educational excellence.

Our online courses are:

 Aligned with **teaching competency frameworks**

 Written by experts in education, including Hachette Learning authors (formerly John Catt)

 Created to enable educators to **develop competencies** linked to their professional development aspirations

 Powered by adaptive learning, to accommodate a diverse range of skills, knowledge and understanding

 Designed to support **effective learning and high-impact teaching**

www.hachettelearning.com/academy